Environmental Education at the Early Childhood Level

Ruth A. Wilson, Editor

Chase Collection

Center for Environmental Education

Antioch New England Graduate School Library

wood engraving by Randy Miller

NAAEE

NORTH AMERICAN
ASSOCIATION FOR
ENVIRONMENTAL
EDUCATION

Printed on recycled paper

ISBN 1-884-008-14-3

THE NORTH AMERICAN ASSOCIATION
FOR ENVIRONMENTAL EDUCATION

NAAEE is a network of professionals and students working in the field of environmental education throughout North America and in over 40 countries around the world. For more than 20 years, the Association has promoted environmental education and supported the work of environmental educators.

There are many environmental interest groups, and many organizations dedicated to the improvement of education. NAAEE uniquely combines and integrates both of these perspectives, taking a positive, cooperative, nonconfrontational approach to promoting education about environmental issues.

The Association is made up of people who have thought seriously—over lifetimes—about how people become literate concerning environmental issues. NAAEE members believe education must go beyond consciousness-raising about these issues. It must prepare people to think together about the difficult decisions they have to make concerning environmental stewardship, and to work together to improve, and try to solve, environmental problems.

NAAEE recognizes the need for a coherent body of information about environmental issues. Its members also recognize that information and analysis are only part of an effective education program. To be truly effective, this body of knowledge must be integrated into all aspects of the curriculum and into all types of educating institutions for the widest array of audiences.

In order to translate theory into reality and provide tangible support for environmental education and environmental educators, NAAEE engages in a variety of programs and activities. Some examples are the annual conference at varying North American sites, an active publications program, the Environmental Education Training Institute, the VINE (Volunteer-led Investigations of Neighborhood Ecology) Network, the Environmental Issues Forums (EIF) program, and the NAAEE Skills Bank.

DEDICATION

To the contributors to this monograph
and the many other dedicated individuals
working to strengthen the bond between
young children and the world of nature.

ACKNOWLEDGMENTS

Support for and contributions to the development of this book have come from many different sources. The contributing authors (listed in the appendix) have been a delight to work with. I relied heavily on their expertise and flexibility and was more than pleased with their contributions and response. Evaluation of the original draft by an expert team of reviewers (Dr. Kathleen Shea Abrams, Florida Department of Education; Dr. Richard Cohen, Pacific Oaks Research Center; and Dr. William Sharp, Roger Tory Peterson Institute) also added greatly to this publication. Their suggestions and support were invaluable in shaping the final version of the manuscript. Also to be acknowledged are the work and support of Barbara Pitman and Judy Braus—dedicated members of the NAAEE (North American Association for Environmental Education) publications committee. Without them, this book could not have moved from the "idea" stage to concrete reality. Thank you, each and every one of you, for your contributions to environmental education at the early childhood level. A special thank you also goes to Gwendolyn Johnson for providing many of the photos throughout this manual and to Shawn Galis for assistance in the preparation of the photos.

Support for the development of this publication was also provided by the Faculty Research Committee of Bowling Green State University, Bowling Green, Ohio. Formatting assistance was provided by Judy Maxey, word processing supervisor, College of Education and Allied Professions, Bowling Green State University.

Contents

Be glad of life because it gives you the chance to love and to work and to play and to look at the stars.

Henry van Dyke

INTRODUCTION

Few people today would question the need for developing an environmentally literate society and the concomitant need for environmental education programs in both formal and nonformal settings. Less well understood, however, is the need to begin environmental education at the early childhood level. The purpose of this publication is to establish a rationale for early childhood environmental education and to offer some guidelines and suggestions for planning and implementing developmentally appropriate environmental education programs for preschool children.

The term "environmental education" as used in this publication is defined as education focusing on the natural environment. Its purpose is to foster not only a cognitive understanding of the natural environment, but also a sense of appreciation and respect for the world of nature.

This monograph is divided into four major sections. Part One outlines the rationale for early childhood environmental education and includes contributions from researchers in both the United States and the United Kingdom. Part Two presents philosophical and research perspectives relating to environmental education for preschool children and outlines some of the major developmental characteristics of children during the early childhood years, especially in relation to cognitive and moral development. Part Three provides specific guidelines and suggestions for developing and implementing environmental education programs at the early childhood level, thus establishing a framework for quality in such programs. Highlighted in Part Four are existing programs offering environmental education for preschool children. These programs include early childhood centers offering a nature-based curriculum and environmental education centers offering preschool programs. While all four sections include contributions from early childhood and environmental education professionals, Part Four is especially diverse in the collage of programs presented. The various sections in Part Four were contributed by preschool teachers, naturalists, program developers, and teacher educators—all eager to share their ideas on the nature and characteristics of environmental education at the early childhood level. Final sections of the monograph offer (a) information on efforts to establish international networking, (b) an annotated list of selected resources, and (c) biographical information on the contributors to the monograph. It is hoped that this monograph will stimulate further interest and provide assistance in developing environmental education programs for preschool children. Readers are invited to become members of the International Network for Environmental Education for Preschoolers and participate in an ongoing dialogue relating to this critical area of environmental education. Please refer to the first part of the Appendix on how to become involved.

*The years of early childhood are the time to prepare
the soil.*

Rachel Carson

I.
Rationale

Pairing Early Childhood Education and Environmental Education
Ruth A. Wilson, Ph.D.

Section Overview

Presented in this section is a discussion by Ruth Wilson on the pairing of early childhood education and environmental education. Also presented are some of the potential benefits associated with such pairing. An earlier version of this section was originally published in The International Journal of Environmental Education and Information (1992).

Early childhood environmental education represents a pairing of early childhood education and environmental education. While these two areas of education each have their own history and unique characteristics, overlap and compatibility between the two have been identified and delineated (Wilson, 1993). Arguments for pairing early childhood education and environmental education address potential benefits for both the natural environment and the young child.

Benefits to the Environment

Environmental education at any level of development is designed to enhance one's understanding of the natural world and to impact positively on attitudes, values, and behaviors. The ultimate goal of environmental education is the development of an environmentally literate and concerned citizenry who will relate to the natural world in a responsible and caring manner. Because many lifelong attitudes

and values are developed early in life, environmental education must start during the early childhood years if it is to have maximum impact.

Many young children today are growing up in a manner that keeps them quite isolated from the world of nature. They are given few opportunities to interact with the natural environment and are thrust into a way of living that shows little respect for the integrity of the natural world. They tend to spend the majority of their time indoors, with only limited opportunities for experiencing and exploring the world of nature. Such children are at risk of never developing a personal bonding with the natural world and may grow up believing that they are "separate from" versus "a part of" the world of nature. They may never develop an awareness of the interrelationship that exists among all living things and may never give much thought to the fact that all their food, air, and water comes from the natural world.

The comments of several young children while on a field trip to a farm suggest they have little understanding of their dependence on the natural world. One little boy, on discovering the source of milk, yelled, "Gross! That's absolutely gross! I will never drink milk again as long as I live." To this, a classmate responded with "I think it's OK. It almost tastes like the real thing." While these comments are somewhat amusing, they are also disturbing. To consider the source of our food "gross" reflects a misunderstanding and a certain prejudice against the natural world—a prejudice that views the world of nature as "dirty," "unrefined," "separate from self," "something to be avoided or kept at a distance," and "something to be tolerated versus respected and enjoyed." Cohen (1984) refers to these attitudes as "anti-nature" and suggests that they are the underlying cause of our social and environmental problems. If we want future generations to care about the natural environment, a change in the way children come to view the world of nature is an absolute necessity. People must understand and care about the natural environment before they will make the necessary decisions and changes in behavior to reverse the rapid deterioration of Planet Earth.

All education is, in one way or another, environmental—that is, the process and content of what we do in our educational programs give messages about the natural environment and our relationship to it. These messages may be positive or negative; rarely are they entirely neutral. Stories read to children speak of the environment—sometimes in very negative ways. Consider the story of Little Red Riding Hood, for example. In this story, Little Red Riding Hood is told not to venture off the path as she travels through the woods to visit her grandmother. The woods is presented as a dangerous, uninviting place. A wolf enters the story and is characterized as an evil, cunning creature with intentions to trick and harm. There's also a woodsman in the story, who becomes a hero because he slays the wolf. While the story of Little Red Riding Hood was probably not written to teach children about the natural environment, the messages are there, nonetheless. There's a message about the natural world as something to be feared and avoided. There's a message about overpowering the natural world through force and violence and, in the process, becoming a hero.

Educational programs that keep children indoors most of the time also give children messages about the world of nature. These messages may suggest that the natural environment is not very important, or that contact with the natural world has little value. It doesn't take long for children to internalize these messages and, later in life, to structure a way of living that reflects the messages they received during their early childhood years.

It's generally understood that hopes for creating an ecologically responsible society rest to a great extent on our ability to change the way we educate our children (Iozzi, 1989; Tokar, 1987). If we are to preserve the natural environment, it becomes imperative that educational programs—from preschool through adulthood—foster a sensitivity to the beauty of nature and an attitude of caring about what happens to Planet Earth. If these attitudes are developed while children are still quite young, the potential for influencing later attitudes and behaviors are greatly enhanced. Environmental education at the early childhood level, then, can serve as the first step in the development of an environmentally literate and concerned citizenry, with great potential for improving the way we, as a society, relate to the natural world (Wilson, 1992).

Benefits to the Child

Young children need frequent positive experiences with nature not only to grow in understanding and appreciation of what the natural world is like, but also to grow in the understanding of who they are. Because we, as human beings, are a part of nature, we will never fully arrive at self-realization until we understand our connectedness to the natural world (Miles, 1986/87; Partridge, 1984). Environmental education at the early childhood level can lay the foundation for the development of this understanding (Burrus-Bammel & Bammel, 1990; Wilson, 1992).

Environmental education at the early childhood level can also foster the overall development of young children. Aesthetic development is one of the areas in which nature can make an especially valuable contribution, in that nature nurtures one's sense of wonder (Carson, 1956; Miles, 1986/87) and leads to an appreciation of beauty (Wilson, 1991). A sense of wonder and an appreciation of beauty are important for quality of life and for perspective on the human relationship to nature (Carson, 1956; Miles, 1986/87).

Environmental education at the early childhood level can also foster a sense of wholeness—that is, an understanding of ourselves as integrated physical, mental, emotional, and spiritual beings (Miles, 1986/87). This sense of wholeness, Miles says, will help the child "along the path toward full personhood" (p. 36). Findings from a review of the empirical literature on the impact of outdoor education by Crompton and Sellar (1981) lend support to the value of environmental education for fostering wholeness. Their findings indicate that environmental education experiences, especially those involving direct contact with the out-of-doors, tend to facilitate positive affective development, along with development in the other domains.

Positive experiences with nature offer a number of benefits to the developing child. "Nature nourishes our emotions, our temperament, our minds, and our souls (Partridge, 1984, p. 109). It's sad, then, that many young children spend most of their time indoors—far removed from direct, positive experiences with the natural world. Studies done in the early 1980s indicate that the average American spends over 95% of his or her time indoors (Cohen, 1984). This situation is, indeed, cause for concern and

lends support to the importance of environmental education at the early childhood level. "To be healthy and fulfilled, we cannot be isolated from the elements and the context which nurtured us" (Partridge, 1984, p. 110).

Another concern has to do with the large numbers of children living in appallingly unhealthy conditions, where poverty, pollution, and crime keep them from experiencing and enjoying the beauty and wonder of the natural world. As these children grow into adulthood, their lack of positive experiences with nature can result in serious misunderstandings about the natural world and a profound indifference toward environmental issues (Wilson, 1992). Providing quality environmental education experiences at the early childhood level—which include frequent opportunities for positive experiences in the natural world—is one avenue that might be used to counterbalance some of the negative influences of poverty and pollution.

Defining Early Childhood Environmental Education

Environmental education at the early childhood level means more than simplifying the activities and experiences of what is typically offered for school-age children in their environmental education programs. The preschool child's perception of the world and his or her way of learning differ considerably from that of older children (Bredekamp, 1987; Cohen & Horm-Wingerd, 1993; Wilson, 1993). To be appropriate, learning activities must reflect these differences. While some work has been done in the field of environmental education to articulate the importance of matching educational experiences to the developmental levels of the learners (Kellert, 1985; Minnesota Department of Education, 1989; Rejeski, 1982; Sebba, 1991; Towler &

Dittmer, 1977), the most definitive articulation of how to plan developmentally appropriate programs for young children is through the National Association for the Education of Young Children (Bredekamp, 1987). Environmental educators would do well to familiarize themselves with these guidelines for early childhood education.

Early childhood educators, on the other hand, would do well to familiarize themselves with ideas on how to infuse environmental education concepts and activities into all aspects of their curriculum. For this, early childhood educators can turn to selected resources from the environmental education literature, including Rachel Carson's <u>The Sense of Wonder</u>. Other suggestions, which may be helpful to both early childhood educators and environmental educators, are offered in the Appendix of this publication.

Summary

There are at least three compelling reasons why environmental education should be offered at the early childhood level: (a) interaction with the natural environment enriches learning and enhances quality of life, (b) students at all developmental levels should have a basic understanding of the natural environment, and (c) the environment matters. While these arguments for environmental education were first articulated as a rationale for environmental education at any level of development (Sankey, 1992), they are certainly applicable to the early childhood level. Several basic understandings lend additional support to environmental education during the preschool years. These understandings are

- The natural environment exists.
- Humans are a part of and dependent upon the natural environment.

- The actions of humans have a profound impact on the natural environment.
- "The environment is something to learn FROM, learn ABOUT, and be responsive TO" (Sankey, 1992, p.9).
- Early positive experiences with the natural environment can have a lasting impact on one's attitudes, values, and behaviors (Wilson, 1993).

Environmental education at the early childhood level has the potential for enhancing the lives of young children, the quality of life for future generations, and the well-being of the natural environment. This potential warrants the attention of not only environmental education professionals and early childhood educators, but the larger society as well.

References

Bredekamp, S. (Ed.). (1987). <u>Developmentally appropriate practice in early childhood programs servicing children from birth through age eight</u>. Washington, DC: National Association for the Education of Young Children.

Burrus-Bammel, L., & Bammel, G. (1990). Outdoor/environmental education—An overview for the wise use of leisure. <u>JOPERD, 61</u> (4), 49-54.

Carson, R. (1956). <u>The sense of wonder</u>. New York: Harper & Row.

Cohen, M. (1984). <u>Prejudice against nature</u>. Freeport, ME: Cobblesmith.

Cohen, S., & Horm-Wingerd, D. (1993). Ecological awareness among preschool children. <u>Environment and Behavior, 25</u> (1), 103-120.

Crompton, J. L., & Sellar, C. (1981). Do outdoor education experiences contribute to positive development in the affective domain? <u>Journal of Environmental Education, 12</u> (4), 21-29.

Iozzi, L. A. (1989). What research says to the educator. Part Two: Environmental education and the affective domain. Journal of Environmental Education, 20 (4), 6-13.

Kellert, S. R. (1985). Attitudes toward animals: Age-related development among children. Journal of Environmental Education, 16 (3), 29-39.

Miles, J. C. (1986/87). Wilderness as a learning place. Journal of Environmental Education, 18 (2), 33-40.

Minnesota Department of Education (1989). Environmental Education. St. Paul, MN: Minnesota Department of Education.

Partridge, E. (1984, Summer). Nature as a moral resource. Environmental Ethics, 6, pp. 101-130.

Rejeski, D. W. (1982). Children look at nature: Environmental perception and education. Journal of Environmental Education, 13 (4), 27-40.

Sankey, K. (1992). A year of opportunity—(or will it be next year?). In S. R. Sterling (Ed.), Annual Review of Environmental Education. Reading, United Kingdom, Council for Environmental Education, pp. 8-10.

Sebba, R. (1991). The landscapes of childhood: The reflection of childhood's environment in adult memories and in children's attitudes. Environment and Behavior, 23 (4), 395-422.

Tokar, B. (1987). The green alternative. San Pedro: R. & E. Miles.

Towler, J., & Dittmer, S. (1977). Psychological readiness and environmental education. In R.H. McCabe (Ed.). Current Issues in Environmental Education—II. Columbus, OH: The ERIC Center for Science, Mathematics, and Environmental Education, pp. 179-83.

Wilson, R. A. (1991). The inclusion of aesthetics. LD Forum, 16 (4), 28-29.

Wilson, R. A. (1992). The importance of environmental education at the early childhood level. International Journal of Environmental Education and Information, 12 (1), 15-24.

Wilson, R. A. (1993). Fostering a sense of wonder during the early childhood years. Columbus, OH: Greyden Press.

Why Nature Education Should Be a Part
of Early Childhood Education
Richard Cohen, Ph.D.
Director, Research Center at Pacific Oaks College

Nature education is critically important in an early childhood program for three reasons:

First, nature education is important for its own sake. The natural world has inspired awe and wonder in human beings for more generations than we can count. Yet children today, especially urban children, are increasingly divorced from or frightened by this wonder, unaware of its power and beauty.

Second, in a world increasingly threatened by the effects of human behavior, we need a custodial generation of young people committed to finding solutions to ecological problems.

Third, nature is a wonderful early childhood curriculum area. The natural world is patterned, yet ever-changing. Birth, growth, and death—topics of abiding interest to young children's opening minds—are central to it. And the observation, classification, and communication skills that develop in the study of nature lead to the skills and dispositions children will need to succeed in school.

The Critical Learning Years for Environmental Education
Daniella Tilbury, Ph.D.

Section Overview

Presented in this section is a discussion of why the early years are so critical for the environmental education of the child. Also offered are some ideas on how to provide environmental education at the early childhood level in a way that best meets the environmental education goals for young children while, at the same time, promoting the social-emotional, cognitive, and moral development needs of preschool children. This section is presented by Taniella Tilbury, who is a professor at the University of Cambridge in the United Kingdom.

The young learners develop most of their final adult physio-neurological capacity quite early in life and therefore learning, especially of attitudes and values so important for the imaginative action in environmental problems, is vital and needs to be considered carefully early in these sequences of life-long learning.
(UNESCO, 1977a, p. 88)

Recognizing the Importance of the Early Years

The importance of the early learning years of a child's education has been grossly underestimated. These learning years can prove to be critical for the environmental education of the child. They mark a period of rapid growth for children in terms of their cognitive, social-emotional, and moral development. Some evidence suggests that teaching in the early years of schooling often underrates children's capabilities. By underestimating the potential of young children, we limit their thinking by our own (Hicks & Fisher, 1985).

The early learning years are a fundamental period for the formation of environmental attitudes and thus of great consequence to environmental education. Attitudes towards the environment are acquired very early in life (Carson, 1978; Gayford, 1987; Hicks & Fisher, 1985; Meakins, 1982; Stapp, 1978; UNESCO, 1977b). Stapp (1978) contends that environmental attitudes learned during the early years are hard to alter and believes that values need to be challenged at this stage before they become deeply entrenched without any serious consideration. Only such an approach, he argues, will develop a generation that is conscious of the need to respect, as well as protect, the environment. Others, like Gayford (1987), point to the early childhood years as critical for the development of environmental commitment.

The existence of "critical" or "sensitive" periods in development is incontrovertibly established (Callaway, 1970; Kellmer-Pringle, 1986). If young children do not receive sufficient stimulation during certain critical or sensitive periods, they are at risk of never achieving their potential in those particular areas of development (e.g., language development, social development, emotional development, etc.). Many have also recognized how environmental experience in the critical phase of the early learning years can determine subsequent development in environmental education

(Carson, 1978; Gayford, 1987; Hicks & Fisher, 1985; Meakins, 1982; Stapp, 1978; UNESCO, 1977b; Williams, 1985). Underestimating the importance of this educational stage can affect the chances of ever achieving the goals of environmental education.

Establishing an Approach

If teaching is oversimplified, children's real learning needs are not effectively addressed. This can occur to the point of not only stunting individual potential, but also leading to children becoming confused and inadequate (Coward, 1990; Kellmer-Pringle, 1986; Storm, 1990/91). In the context of environmental education, Coward (1990) reports how, as a result of superficial coverage of environmental work, pupils do not become fully aware of the complexity of issues. In certain cases, she argues, children may resort to "shaming" adults about their lifestyles over issues of which children have only a simplistic and often inaccurate understanding.

Since the early years of schooling offer tremendous opportunities to facilitate the child's understanding and appreciation of the environment, a sound and clear understanding of an appropriate approach is critical. Environmental education programs for young children should reflect an understanding of the early years as fundamental to the social-emotional, cognitive, and moral development of the individual. Such programs should provide opportunities for children to

(1) Experience the environment firsthand and explore their personal relationship with it
(2) Experience social interaction, group work, drama, and role play
(3) Develop a sense of membership in society through the study of environmental concerns
(4) Analyze and discuss their environmental fears and feelings, as well as those of other groups and cultures
(5) Develop a growing understanding of other people's needs and rights
(6) Develop a global perspective of environmental problems
(7) Foster an awareness of the individual's place and responsibilities in the local and global community and of his or her role in maintaining and improving environmental quality
(8) Introduce children to real (i.e., meaningful) environmental issues

Summary

The quality of environmental education during the early childhood years is significant both for the development of the child and the management and protection of the environment. It is therefore crucial that the environmental learning needs and abilities of young children be effectively addressed.

References

Callaway, R. W. (1970). Modes of biological adaptation—Their role in international development. Perceptual Cognitive Development Monographs, 1 (1). USA: The Galton Institute.

Carson, S. (1978). Environmental education—Principles and practice. London: Edward Arnold.

Coward, R. (1990, May 25). Greening the child. New Statesman.

Gayford, C. (1987). Training and education in relation to environmental problems. Annual Review of Environmental Education, No. 1. Council of Environmental Education.

Hicks, D., & Fisher, S. (1985). World studies 8-13. A teachers handbook. Edinburgh: Oliver & Boyd.

Kellmer-Pringle, M. (1986). The needs of children. London: Idalgo.

Meakins, D. (1982). Harvesting one-hundredfold. Kenya: United Nations Environment Programme (UNEP).

Stapp, W. (1978). An instructional model for environmental education. <u>Prospects, 8</u> (4), 495-507.

Storm, M. (1990/91). Evangelical approach to environmental education. <u>Annual Review of Environmental Education</u>, No. 4. Council of Environmental Education, pp. 31-32.

UNESCO (1977a). <u>Needs and priorities in environmental education: An international survey.</u> ENVED No. 6. Paris: UNESCO.

UNESCO (1977b). <u>Final report: Tbilisi UNESCO</u>. October 14-26, 1977, DOC UNESCO/UNED MP/49. Paris: UNESCO.

Williams, R. (1985). <u>Environmental education and teacher education project, 1984-1987</u>. World Wildlife Fund.

The care of rivers is not a question of rivers, but of the human heart.

Tanaka Shozo, <u>Listening to Nature</u>

II.

Philosophical and Research Perspectives

Children's Environmental Knowledge
Stewart Cohen, Ph.D.

Section Overview

Presented in this section is a brief review of the literature relating to children's environmental knowledge—what it is and how it might be fostered. This section was developed by Dr. Stewart Cohen, who is involved in research on ecological awareness in young children.

The Study of Children's Environmental Knowledge

Learning to act with respect for natural settings and acquiring a sense of reverence towards the environment is a life-long process. Correspondingly, it would appear that early educational training in appropriate pedagogical settings would be a critical arena for initiating environmental education. And, in fact, a multitude of materials and programs have been developed in response to this challenge. Yet, the database upon which educational efforts need be grounded has not been established, leading to a diversity of learning outcomes. There are several reasons why our efforts fall short.

Scientific interest in children's understanding of ecologically based issues is a relatively uncharted area of study. Correspondingly, there are significant gaps in our knowledge of how children become interested in their environment: particularly, how their concern for their environment originates, the course and development of their environmental interests, and how ac-

quired attitudes toward the environment become translated into ecologically viable practices (Hart & Chawla, 1981).

Where researchers have studied children's knowledge of environmental systems, these studies have been conducted among older, middle school children, not preschool or early elementary school children. Unfortunately, few studies have actually been performed with very young children, although preliminary evidence now suggests that environmental education may be directed toward fostering ecological interests in young children (Cohen & Horm-Wingerd, 1993).

The largest single body of young children's understanding of physical systems is derived from the work of Piaget (1954, 1960a, 1960b). While Piaget was not directly interested in children's awareness of ecological issues, his findings nevertheless do offer some important scientific and pedagogical insights associated with children's ecological understandings. According to Piagetian theory, the young child's view of the world and his or her mental capabilities differ greatly from those of older children and adults. The child develops the cognitive abilities of an adult by progressing through a series of stages, each of which is characterized by a particular type of mental ability. The following table is a brief outline of these stages.

PIAGET'S STAGES OF COGNITIVE DEVELOPMENT

Stage	Characteristics	Approximate Age
sensori-motor	sensory perceptions motor activity	0-2 years
preoperational	mental egocentricity prelogical reasoning	2-7 years
concrete operational	thinking dependent on concrete vs. abstract or hypothetical terms	7-11 years
formal operations	abstract, hypothetical thought	11+ years

Piaget found that between three and eleven years of age children undergo dramatic changes in their perceptions of the world. Among very young children, for example, early cognition reflects **animistic thought**, viz., attributing life to objects found in nature that, while inanimate, possess some of the characteristics of animate life, such as movement (e.g., stones, clouds, the wind). For example, a young child may move stones out of her path so that they won't be stepped upon and, subsequently, be injured. In addition, Piaget argued that young children are also **egocentric** in their thought, viz., believe that there is only one perspective of events and that all observers share the same point of view. For example, a child observing his sand castle collapse with the incoming tide may remark to his parents, "The earth is falling down."

According to Piaget, two cognitive processes, each of which contributes to the acquisition of an ecological perspective, emerge to assist children in the development of a more objective perspective. First, through varied sharing of cooperative and related social interactions, children begin to perceive that others may hold differing or alternative points of view. This evolving recognition of different perspectives aids

children in the development of a sense of **reciprocity**. While initially children's focus of reciprocity is limited, over time reciprocity increases and broadens. Within this sphere it is children's maturing awareness of reciprocal arrangements that enables them to examine their specific views relative to those held by others.

Concurrent with the emergence of a reciprocal perspective, children acquire a sense of **relativity**. Increasingly, events become viewed as relational and interdependent. In an ecological context, just as children become aware of themselves within the sphere/influence/context of involvements with others, children are now capable of noting the interrelationships between plant and animal life forms, as well as progressively more intricate actions and reactions that affect/control ecosystems at work. This balancing of cognitive processes, which reflects an increasing awareness of cause-effect relations, suggests an agenda of events for children that may enhance their ecological perspective of the environment.

Creating an Ecologically Based Learning Environment

Hungerford and Volk (1990) argue that "If environmental issues are to become an integral part of instruction designed to change behavior, instruction must go beyond an 'awareness' or 'knowledge' of issues. Students must be given an opportunity to develop a sense of 'ownership' and 'empowerment' so that they are fully invested in an environmental sense and prompted to become responsible, active citizens" (p.17).

Experiences designed to foster children's awareness of environmental issues, to assist in their acquisition of sound ecological practices, and to enhance better understandings of the human/Earth interrelationship should be research based and predicated upon sound pedagogical principles. In young children, ecologically based learning should be **developmentally appropriate, occur across real settings,** and **involve children's active participation.**

Creating developmentally appropriate programs for young learners requires a match between the child's cognitive status and the demands of the environmental curriculum. It is clear that issues of ecological interest are most often temporally removed from the child's immediate experience (i.e., evolving over significant periods of time, rather than within a given lifetime), globally divergent (i.e., appearing at distances far removed from the child's immediate life space), geologically divergent (i.e., appear in varying forms of complexity), and frequently far removed from the child's actual realm of life experiences (Issacs, 1930; Chawla & Hart, 1988). In terms of ecological understandings, however, preoperational (i.e., preschool) children appear most able to benefit from experiences that are continuous rather than transitory, that are stable rather than in flux, that are concrete rather than abstract, and that are personally rather than conceptually meaningful.

A second characteristic of an ecologically based learning environment for young children is that it provide for real interactions with nature. A number of studies involving children's attitudes toward technology and nature (Bunting & Cousins, 1985), environmental use and morality (Issacs, 1930), and relations between rural versus urban place of residence (Dyar, 1975; Kellert, 1985) demonstrate that real involvement in nature is an important component in fostering children's ecological understandings. Other researchers (Blades, 1989; Sebba, 1991) concur with Goldbeck and

Liben's (1988) observation that "the means of acquiring knowledge about the environment is through direct interaction with the environment" (p.51).

A third idea important in facilitating scientific and ecologically based learning in young children is the notion of active participation (Cohen, 1989; Trostle & Cohen, 1989; Bredekamp, 1987). In ecological education, this concept gains support from the longitudinal study of a child's development of scientific knowledge (Navarra, 1955), children's understanding of the hydrologic cycle (Kates & Katz, 1977), their involvement in agricultural activities (Harvey, 1989), and in terms of their acquisition of environmentally responsible behavior (Ramsey, Hungerford, & Tomera, 1981). From these studies it is apparent that ecological knowledge is heavily dependent upon participatory interactions with both living things and physical systems (Chawla & Hart, 1988).

While it's true that environmental education from preschool through adulthood should reflect the basic principles of (1) being developmentally appropriate, (2) occurring across real settings, and (3) involving active participation, the challenge at the early childhood level is providing such experiences in the context of what is meaningful to young children. The stages of cognitive development, as outlined by Piaget, can provide a "best practices" framework for planning environmental education activities and experiences for the preschool child.

References

Blades, M. (1989). Children's ability to learn about the environment from direct experience and from spatial representations. Children's Environments Quarterly, 6, 4-14.

Bredekamp, S. (1987). <u>Developmentally appropriate practice in early childhood programs serving children from birth through age eight</u>. Expanded edition. Washington, DC: National Association for the Education of Young Children.

Bunting, T. E., & Cousins, L. R. (1985). Environmental dispositions among school-age children. <u>Environment and Behavior, 17</u>, 725-68.

Chawla, L., & Hart, R. A. (1988). The roots of environmental concern. In D. Lawrence, R. Habe, A. Hacker, & D. Sherod (Eds.), <u>Paths to coexistence</u>. Washington, DC: Environmental Design Research Association.

Cohen, S. (1989). Fostering shared learning among children and adults: The children's museum. <u>Young Children, 44</u> (4), 20-24.

Cohen, S., & Horm-Wingerd, D. (1993). Children and the environment: Ecological awareness among preschool children. <u>Environment and Behavior, 25</u>, 103-20.

Dyar, N. (1975). Assessing the environmental attitudes and behaviors of a seventh grade school population. Ph.D. thesis, University of California, Los Angeles.

Goldbeck, S. L., & Liben, S. (1988). A cognitive-developmental approach to children's representations of the environment. <u>Children's Environments Quarterly, 5</u>, 46-53.

Harvey, M. R. (1989). Children's experience with vegetation. <u>Children's Environments Quarterly, 6</u>, 36-43.

Hart, R. A., & Chawla, L. (1981). The development of children's concern for the environment. In N. Watts & J. Wohlwill (Eds.), <u>Environmental Psychology</u> (special issue), <u>Zeitschrift fur Unwelpolitik, 4</u> International Institute for Environment and Society, Berlin.

Hungerford, H. R., & Volk, T. L. (1990). Changing learner behavior through environmental education. <u>Journal of Environmental Education, 22</u> (3), 8-21.

Issacs, S. (1930). <u>Intellectual growth in young children</u>. New York: Harcourt, Brace.

Kates, R. W., & Katz, C. (1977). The hydrologic cycle and the wisdom of the child. <u>Geographic Review, 67</u> (1), 51-62.

Kellert, S. R. (1985). Attitudes toward animals: Age-related development among children. <u>Journal of Environmental Education, 16</u> (3), 29-39.

Navarra, J. G. (1955). <u>The development of scientific concepts in a young child</u>. New York: Columbia University Bureau of Publications.

Piaget, J. (1954). <u>The construction of reality in the child</u>. New York: Basic Books.

Piaget, J. (1960a). <u>Judgment and reasoning in the child</u>. New York: Harcourt & Brace.

Piaget, J. (1960b). <u>The child's conception of physical causality</u>. Totowa, New Jersey: Littlefield, Adams, Patterson.

Ramsey, J.; Hungerford, H. R.; & Tomera, A. N. (1981). The effects of environmental action and environmental case study instruction on eighth grade students. <u>Journal of Environmental Education, 13</u> (1), 24-29.

Sebba, R. (1991). The landscapes of childhood. The reflection of childhood's environment in adult memories and in children's attitudes. <u>Environment and Behavior, 23</u>, 395-422.

Trostle, S. L., & Cohen, S. (1989). Big, bigger, biggest . . . when mammoths walked the earth: Discovering dinosaurs. <u>Childhood Education, 65</u> (3), 140-45.

Young Children and Environmental Ethics
Mavis Lewis-Webber

> **Section Overview**
> This section is based on the premise that the building blocks for developing responsible citizens must be established during the preschool years. A description of the "ideal" environmentally responsible adult is provided, along with a discussion of how an understanding of children's moral and cognitive development can be used to aid the growth of environmental ethics in young children. The section concludes with some guiding principles for fostering environmental values at the early childhood level. This section was developed by Mavis Lewis-Webber, author of <u>Earthcycles: Environmental Education with Preschool Children</u>.

We do not inherit the earth from our ancestors—we borrow it from our children.

This popular phrase puts a great deal of responsibility on present generations not only to leave the earth in working order, but to instill an environmental ethic in their children to ensure the Earth, as we know it, will be a beautiful place for generations to come. Not only do we strive for a beautiful Earth, but also one that will sustain us with clean air, land and water. It is in part because of this concern for future generations that educating oneself and others regarding environmental issues has become very necessary. Media portrayals of children in classrooms learning about environmental issues are fairly common. Adults have ac-

cess to environmental education through a variety of media, including university offerings, the news media, etc. However, there are few initiatives involving preschool children.

If people begin to value the natural environment at a very young age, a concern for sustainable development of natural resources will begin to develop. However, because young children develop values through adult direction, it is imperative that parents and child care professionals are informed regarding environmental issues. Institutions that train child care professionals need to include an environmental component in their curriculum. Parenting courses should also discuss the importance of beginning to instill an environmental ethic in preschool children.

This section will not discuss the importance of educating adults. The assumption is made that adults recognize their vital role in developing an environmental ethic in preschool children. It is acknowledged that this is not necessarily the case in reality, and that the adults, as well as young children, will always benefit from additional learning experiences.

"As we now know for certain that the ecological results of many of our current habits will be visited, unwanted, on future generations, it seems congruent with our moral institutions to say we ought to change our ways to spare our descendents" (Taylor, 1986, p. 80). Not only must we change our ways, we must instill a moral attitude with a respect for nature in our children.

The group identified as crucial to begin the process of education is preschool children, as the direction of the future will one day be in their hands. In addition, it is recognized that a large portion of an individual's development, including the establishment of the foundations for future developments, occurs at a very young age.

Defining an Environmental Ethic

For the state of the Earth to improve, or at least stay status quo, a change must come about. This change must begin in our value system. An environmental ethic and a respect for nature must permeate our decision making and be reflected in our daily activities. A tall order, perhaps, but less intimidating than the anticipated environmental crisis future generations may face.

An environmental ethic might be defined as a respect for nature that permeates a person's character, personality, and life. Individuals with an established environmenal ethic would be guided by this ethic in terms of the personal choices they need to make on a daily basis—from where they do their grocery shopping to where they invest their money. In making their decisions, they would "deliberate correctly about what action ought to be done and . . . carry out the decision resulting from that deliberation" (Taylor, 1986, p. 88).

As actions are an indicator of values, prior thought and consideration must be given to how personal behavior reflects upon a value system. "What is necessary, along with continued reliance on technology to help solve environmental problems, is the recognition that our behavior patterns and value systems need to change" (Shrader-Frechette, 1981, p. 16).

"An ethic appropriate for our time can be stated in terms of the 'beautiful' and all-encompassing concept that implies not only a moral conception of man and of principles respecting relations among men but also understanding by which to judge the acceptability of environmental modification, enhancement, and general use. Such an ethic can be expressed as follows: Every person shall strive to protect and enhance the beautiful everywhere his or her impact is felt, and to maintain or increase the functional diversity of the environment in general" (Hanson, 1986, pp. 27-28). Protecting the beautiful includes everything from encouraging birds to make your backyard their home, to helping people in a third world country apply the concept of sustainable development to their own lives.

The "ideal" environmentally responsible citizen is one who has developed a moral attitude that reflects a respect for nature. An environmental ethic would reflect in a person's moral attitude, behavior, and value system such that daily choices and decisions would be affected.

Developing an Environmental Ethic

Stages of cognitive development and moral development are intertwined and both influence an individual's environmental ethic. The work of Piaget and Kohlberg is pertinent to this discussion and supports the need to foster an environmental ethic at an early age. Kohlberg, building on the theories of Piaget, outlined moral development in a series of levels. These levels are described as follows:

Level	Characteristics
Level 1 Preconventional	Rules are followed to avoid punishment
Level 2 Conventional	Rules are followed in respect for authority
Level 3 Postconventional	Behavior is based on self-chosen principles

Successful completion of level 1 is necessary to move to level 2 and so on. Preschool children can be expected to be moving toward completion of level 1 in preparation for advancement into level 2.

Moral development tends to move to a higher level in conjunction with cognitive development, yet for many individuals moral development does not keep pace with logical reasoning. That is, "there is a parallelism between an individual's logical stage and his moral stage. Many individuals are at a higher logical stage than the parallel moral stage, but essentially none are at a higher moral stage than their logical stage" (Lickona, 1976, p. 32).

Kohlberg concluded "that a moral sense is not acquired simply through the acceptance of society's rules as taught by precept, punishment, or identification with respected figures. He found that it also involves an internal, personal series of changes in social attitudes" (Ambron, 1981, pp. 416-17). The foundation of a moral sense, however, is laid in level 1 and built upon as children mature. As preschool children are in the preconventional level of moral development (which is concerned with avoiding damage to persons and property), this is a perfect opportunity to encourage respect for the natural environment.

With increasing cognitive maturation, children are able to move on to levels 2 and 3 of moral development. The ultimate goal in the development of an environmental ethic is to operate out of level 3, where individuals are clear about their values and uphold principles that are not in conflict with each other. As stated earlier, the sooner young children participate in activities with an environmental theme, the more likely they are to have a strong environmental ethic as part of their value system. The challenge exists for parents and professionals to provide learning activities that are appropriate to the child's developmental level.

Planning Developmentally Appropriate Activities

A child's cognitive level of functioning determines, to a large extent, the kinds of activities that are developmentally appropriate for that child. According to Piaget, children's cognitive development progresses through four major stages: sensorimotor, preoperational, concrete operational, and formal operations. It is at the formal operational stage that individuals can formulate principles of behavior reflecting on their value systems. While all people should strive to achieve this goal, the focus of this section is how to encourage children toward higher levels of cognitive and moral development.

Preschool children (two to five years old) are in the preoperational stage of development, which is characterized by the child who "still lacks the ability to think about problems or to perform mental operations without having to perform actual physical operations" (Arbuthnot & Faust, 1978, p. 36). The educational implication is to plan learning activities around hands-on involvement. Another major characteristic of this stage of development is the ability to "represent" or use symbols. This ability is reflected in the child's gradual attainment of language. Children in this stage are eager to verbally label objects in their environment. Thus, a perfect opportunity is presented to lay the groundwork of environmental knowledge.

Adult direction or guidance during the preoperational stage is important to both the child's cognitive and moral development. This direction is best provided through opportunities for active involvement and the fostering of language.

Fostering an Environmental Ethic

Environmental education includes "the process of recognizing values and clarifying concepts in order to develop skills and attitudes necessary to understand and appreciate the inter-relatedness among man, his culture and his biophysical surroundings" (Carson, 1978, p. viii). As young children are active people, their curiosity, trust, and desire to learn will assist the process of clarifying concepts and exploring interrelatedness between facets of the environment. Current research in early childhood education suggests that children's basic attitudes toward life, their approach to new experiences, and their feelings about themselves and others are established in the first few years of life. It is safe to assume that their attitudes toward the environment are forming then as well (Rockwell, Sherwood, & Williams, 1983).

Adults have a critical role to play in fostering an environmental ethic in young children. They should start by providing children with opportunities to use their senses in exploring the natural environment and observing how it functions. Adults should also use language to extend the learning experience. Adults can sharpen children's observational skills by talking about details while an object is being inspected. For example, bird names and their habits, where they live and what they like to eat, and the sound of their calls are all details that are of interest to young children.

One concept that can begin in a simplistic form and become more complex, depending upon the children's capabilities, is the notion that living and nonliving material has a beginning and an end—or a life cycle. For example, the children can be involved in planting a tomato seed, caring for it, reaping the harvest, putting the exhausted plant in a composter, and then using the compost for fertilizing the garden.

Interrelatedness of objects in the natural environment is an important concept to be introduced to children. While the young child will not develop a full understanding of this concept, the introduction to it provides a strong foundation upon which further development can be built.

With knowledge develops respect. The theme of respect ought to permeate all practical applications of instilling an environmental ethic in preschool children. Respect for people, animals, plants, birds, and inanimate objects is a valuable attitude upon which to build a lifelong environmental ethic. In addition to respecting and seeing the beautiful in the world around them, it is equally important that people value and care for all aspects of the environment. The world needs people who may not necessarily love snakes, but who appreciate the role they play in the environment (Rockwell, Sherwood, & Williams, 1983).

Environmental education and the fostering of an environmental ethic are interactive, sharing processes. An adult's enthusiasm and respect for the natural environment will determine, in large part, to what extent young children develop a moral attitude with a respect for the natural environment. It's important for the process to begin while children are still very young. What better gift can we as parents and teachers give this precarious Earth than a generation of children who have learned to know and love the natural world (Rockwell, Sherwood, & Williams, 1983)?

References

Ambron, S. R. (1981). Child development. 3rd ed. New York: Holt, Rinehart, & Winston.

Arbuthnot, J. B., & Faust, D. (1978). Teaching moral reasoning: Theory and practice. New York: Holt, Rinehart, & Winston.

Carson, S. (Ed.) (1978). <u>Environmental education: Principles and practice</u>. London: Edward Arnold Publishers.

Hanson, P. P. (Ed.). (1986). <u>Environmental ethics: Philosophical and policy perspectives</u>. Burnaby, BC: Simon Fraser University.

Lickona, T. (Ed.). (1976). <u>Moral development and behavior: Theory, research and social issues</u>. New York: Holt, Rinehart, & Winston.

Rockwell, R. E.; Sherwood, E. A.; & Williams, R. A. (1983). <u>Hug-A-Tree: And other things to do outdoors with young children</u>. Mt. Rainier, MD: Gryphon House.

Shrader-Frechette, K. S. (1981). <u>Environmental ethics</u>. Pacific Grove, CA: The Boxwood Press.

Taylor, P. W. (1986). <u>Respect for nature: A theory of environmental ethics</u>. Princeton: University Press.

Rachel Carson: A Mentor for Early Childhood Environmental Education
Robert E. Holtz, Ed.D.

Section Overview

Presented in this section is a proposal by the author that Rachel Carson be considered the patron saint, or mentor, for early childhood environmental education. Arguments in support of this proposal and an introduction to Rachel Carson's book, <u>The Sense of Wonder,</u> are also provided.

A common mistake made in elementary and early childhood education is doing what has been or is being done with children two to five years older. Properly modified, such lessons can be successful, but unless adapted to the age level being taught and to the needs of the individuals in the group, frustration of both student and teacher is apt to be painfully obvious.

It's also important to avoid inundating young children with a laundry list of Planet Earth's environmental woes. Young children are not capable of understanding most of the implications of such problems, nor can they begin to grasp the possibilities for resolving the issues related to such problems. Environmental issues are frequently a tangled web of values, attitudes, and options.

An alternate—and more appropriate approach—for early childhood environmental education is to work from RachelCarson's concept of the sense of wonder (Carson, 1956). As a matter of fact,

RachelCarson may be consider ed the patron saint (mentor or model teacher, if "patron saint" is too strong for some) of early childhood environmental education.

Carson never had children of her own, but she raised her grandnephew, Roger, after her sister, Marian, died in 1937 and Marjorie, Marian's daughter and mother of Roger, died in 1957 (McCay, 1993). Carson's relationship to Roger, particularly in terms of her teaching him about the wonders of nature are described in her 1956 book, <u>The Sense of Wonder</u>. This book certainly covers early childhood education, because it begins with a description of Carson taking Roger to the beach at night when he was but twenty months old.

Carson also believed (as do many others) it is not necessary to consciously teach children the names of plants and animals. However, she confesses that she did use names as she described certain things to Roger and then noted later how readily he could recall those names as he remembered the functions of various plants (Carson, 1956, p. 18).

I concur with that approach, because even though names of objects are not the most important thing to be taught, when we later wish to refer to those objects we do need some way to identify (name) such items. If we all use the same identifying name for one particular object then we all can communicate with each other about that object. Therefore, I believe, even though naming an object should not be the first thing we do for children—because they then often feel they need no more information—names do serve a useful purpose for the process of communication.

At this point, some readers may be asking whether we are really speaking about environmental education. I believe we definitely are because I feel young children need to be exposed to the environment in which they live, both the built and the natural. I would also argue that children are in far greater need of a conscientious exposure to the natural environment than the built because many parents never expose their children to the natural environment in a meaningful way, but those children live every day in the built environment. Further, if we as adults can help young children develop a sense of wonder (RachelCarson's philosophy), plus a basic awareness that there is a great diversity of life in nature, they will later find it easier to understand the importance of protecting various habitats for those different living things. We will have helped them develop values (e.g., all living things have a place in nature), which lead to attitudes (we should protect the habitat of organisms which can not do so on their own), and these finally could lead to actions (personal involvement in the struggle to preserve an area or contributing financially to an organization that is attempting to preserve the area).

Anyone who has taken young children into the outdoors knows that children invariably love a nature setting. At times they examine every little organism they notice. At other times they just want to run and shout for joy because of the setting in which they find themselves. Nearly always they pepper you with question after question because nature promotes curiosity. Sometimes they will prefer to just sit quietly to absorb the moment and/or the entire scene. At those times they probably feel

as Roger did when he says, "I'm glad we came" (Carson, 1956, p. 22). What greater reward could a child give to the adult who took him or her into the outdoors, the natural environment?

Rachel Carson's philosophy and feelings concerning early childhood environmental education, and the title for the book, are revealed when she says, "If I had influence with the good fairy who is supposed to preside over the christening of all children I should ask that her gift to each child in the world be a sense of wonder so indestructible that it would last throughout life" (pp. 42-43). She follows up that wish by indicating that even if a child begins life with an "inborn sense of wonder," no good fairy is going to promote it (p. 45). Therefore, she argues, every child will need a minimum of one adult who will share his or her sense of wonder with that child. That, I believe, should be the foundation for our present-day early childhood environmental education.

To those parents and teachers who feel that they can't do this type of early childhood environmental education, I would say, "Don't panic." You don't need to know everything. It certainly is helpful to be able to identify things in nature, but the names aren't critical. It is far more important to simply point out things to children. Once you start doing that, you will be surprised at how much children will point out to you. In many cases, just being the caring, accompanying adult is all you will need to do. RachelCarson takes this even a step further in observing that "it is not half so important to know as to feel" (p.45).

Even though we are speaking of early childhood environmental education, don't we want the same thing for these children as they mature? Don't we want them to feel strongly about such issues as the importance of biodiversity, clean air and water, the value of all living things, etc.? We all probably know individuals who are aware of what is needed to correct our environmental problems, but who have no passion that might lead them to contribute time, talent, or money toward the resolution of the issues contributing to these problems. Their feelings, which contribute to values and attitudes, never developed to the point where they could see such issues as being of much importance or of more importance than pursuing personal pleasure, making money, or maybe something as mundane as watching television.

As one continues to read through The Sense of Wonder, it is easy to see that Carson has other advice for early childhood environmental education. She points out, at least by implication, that it is not costly to develop an early childhood environmental education program—at least not the outdoor portion of it. Carson notes that a simple hand lens makes an excellent piece of equipment for young children wishing to explore the world around them (p. 59).

Carson speaks of smells in nature (p.66) and emphasizes the value of listening to the sounds of nature (pp.68-81). What I infer from those passages is that as educators of young children, we need to remind ourselves of the importance of using all our senses to make observations. Then, in turn, we need to help children also realize the value of using each sense to learn about the natural world. I teach an introductory field biology course for college students. It never fails that during the first or second field trip after I ask "What was that?" in response to some sound I heard, a student will say, "I didn't hear anything." My suspicion is that students respond that way for two reasons. First, very likely adults seldom took that person into the natural world when he or she was a child.

Second, it is also true that most of us live in a setting that has a lot of hustle, bustle, and hectic moments; therefore, we have learned well how to block out many of the distractions surrounding us in order to preserve some inner calm. But when we get outdoors we need to unlearn that technique and once again savor the input coming to all our senses. Of course, we need to remember a few commonsense warnings for some senses in particular, such as not to taste items in nature if you don't know what they are. Many are poisonous. The same goes for touching poison ivy, poison oak, and so on.

A careful reading of The Sense of Wonder will reveal that Rachel Carson never used the words "early childhood" or "environmental education." However, she definitely was speaking about the importance of exposing young children (early childhood) to nature (part of the environment), and she was talking about a type of mentorship (one type of role for an educator). Therefore, I firmly believe The Sense of Wonder should be read and reread by everyone interested in early childhood environmental education. And if we truly believe both that there are environmental problems and that the early years of life are a very critical phase in the development of children, we must realize that environmental education is a must in our early childhood education programs and, likewise, that environmental education programs should include special offerings for preschool children.

References

Carson, R. (1956; rpt. 1984). The sense of wonder. New York: Harper & Row.

McCay, M. A. (1993). Rachel Carson. New York: Twayne Publishers.

. . . the tree has spoken to me with its many tongued leaves . . .

Meridel Le Sueur

III.

Program Development

A Framework for Quality
Ruth A. Wilson, Ph.D.

Section Overview

The purpose of this section is to provide information on how to design an early childhood environmental education program representing "best practices" in both early childhood education and environmental education. Currently, as far as can be determined, there are only a few sites offering early childhood environmental education as an ongoing preschool program (Wilson, 1994). Several of these sites will be mentioned and/or described in this section of the monograph. A further description of early childhood environmental education programs will be presented in Part Four. Following this section, however, are two brief descriptions of programs exemplifying several characteristics of quality programming in early childhood environmental education. These descriptions were written by teachers working in the respective programs.

Introduction

Early childhood environmental education programs can be developed in many different settings—early childhood centers, home day care programs, summer day camps, nature centers, zoos, museums, the backyards of individual families, and a variety of other sites. The setting requires neither a park nor a school. What is required is the opportunity for children to have some direct contact with the natural world (Cole, 1992; James, 1992; Peterson &

Hungerford, 1981; Rejeski, 1982; Wilson, 1993a). The nature and extent of opportunities for direct contact will vary considerably from setting to setting. In some places, a potted vegetable plant and a spider's web may be the primary vehicles for nature exploration. Other places may offer nature trails, a butterfly garden, and a pond. Whatever the site, the potential exists for offering exciting environmental education experiences for young children.

Early childhood environmental education programs may be led by naturalists, preschool teachers, parents, day care providers, and other individuals working with young children. Formal education in environmental science is not required, nor is a degree in early childhood education. Effective leadership in early childhood environmental education is based on an understanding of how young children learn and a sincere interest in the natural world (Rejeski, 1982; Wilson, 1993a). With this understanding and interest, the pairing of young children and nature can result in quality early childhood environmental education programs.

Quality programs, however, require more than a place, a teacher or leader, and a set of activities. Quality programs are built around philosophical, theoretical, and research foundations, and carefully constructed curricular applications. Quality educational programs are driven by a philosophy, a set of beliefs, and specific goals. Activities, materials, and other learning experiences are then provided in accordance with the philosophical orientation of the program. The following is a discussion of some of the components of early childhood education and how these might be structured in developing quality early childhood environmental education experiences for young children.

Statement of Purpose

Many programs start with a statement of purpose. The following statements were developed by three different early childhood environmental education programs, each reflecting best practices in the field.

> *Learning about ourselves and the rest of the world—Nature's Way*
> (Nature's Way Preschool, Kalamazoo, Michigan)

> *To teach the value of interconnectedness of all living things as a way of life*
> (Young Naturalist Center, Studio City, California)

> *Learning to love — both ourselves and the environment*
> (Beginner's Nature Program, New Canaan, Connecticut)

Each of these statements reflects a "groundedness" in the world of nature, and suggests that it is through the natural world and the way of nature that we learn about ourselves, as well. As mentioned earlier, this understanding is strongly supported by the professional literature in both early childhood education (Cohen & Trostle, 1990; Singer,1992) and environmental education (Burrus-Bammel & Bammel, 1990; Henderson, 1990; Kirkby, 1989) and can thus be considered appropriate for programming in early childhood environmental education.

Philosophy

Whether it is formally stated or not, educational programs are driven by a philosophy or set of beliefs. Quality early childhood education programs are based on the philosophy that early childhood is a unique and important phase of life, and that early childhood experiences set the stage for who a person can and will be for the rest of his or her life. The philosophy statements of the Nature's Way Preschool, the Young Naturalist Center, and the Beginner's Nature Program reflect a healthy integration of early childhood education and environmental education.

From Nature's Way Preschool: *We want children to have fun learning about themselves and their natural and man-made surroundings, while becoming aware of their own potential and their relationships to their environments, including other people. Our program combines traditional . . . preschool activities with environmental education programs. Nature's Way Preschools teach the child by providing experiences that develop mind, body, and spirit.*

From the Young Naturalist Center: *Children are encouraged to stay in touch with their inborn sense of wonder, a sense that is their impetus to explore the world around them, to learn to understand and respect the interdependence of all things. . . . At the Young Naturalist Center, children learn because they want to, because their natural curiosity is piqued by what they themselves discover and create in a natural setting.*

From the Beginner's Nature Program: *An exciting part of this unique preschool is that we can and do accomplish environmental education goals while addressing the whole child's developmental needs. We have successfully integrated environmental education into our curriculum, not as a separate subject but rather infused into art, music, pre-math, pre-reading, and other subject areas. Social, emotional, language, perceptual, cognitive, and physical skills are all addressed in this nature-based curriculum.*

Evident in each of these philosophy statements is the understanding that young children learn best when they can have fun while learning and when they're curious about and interested in the learning experiences. Also evident is a concern for the whole child and the child's understanding of his or her relationship to the rest of the world. What makes these programs unusual is the emphasis on the natural environment as both content and setting for the early childhood education program.

Goals and Objectives

In addition to a statement of purpose and a philosophy, specific goals are often used by educational programs to establish consistency and continuity. The following set of goals and related objectives might be used as a framework for an early childhood environmental education program. These goals and objectives were developed from a synthesis of information and ideas from a variety of publications representing both environmental education and early childhood education. Such works include Avoiding Infusion Confusion: A Practical Handbook for Infusing Environmental Activities into Your Classroom (Hayden et al, 1987), Essential Learnings in Environmental Edu-

cation (Hanselman, Raghunathan, & Sarabiihai [Eds.], 1990), Exploring Science in Early Childhood: A Developmental Approach (Lind, 1991), Model Learner Outcomes for Environmental Education (Minnesota Department of Education, 1991), Developmentally Appropriate Practice in Early Childhood Programs Serving Children from Birth through Age Eight (Bredekamp, 1987), Science Experiences for the Early Childhood Years (Harlan, 1988), and Environmental Education in the Schools (Braus& W ood, 1993).

Goal: *To help children become aware of and enjoy the beauty and wonder of the natural world*
Related Objectives:
- To help children see that the world is full of beauty and wonder
- To introduce works of art, music, and literature inspired by various aspects of the natural world
- To help children experience the natural world as a source of personal joy and inspiration

Goal: *To help children become aware of the concepts of cycles, diversity, and interconnectedness in the world of nature*
Related Objectives:
- To help children discover that the world of nature is in a state of constant change and that change is natural and normal
- To help children feel comfortable with changes that occur around them
- To help children discover that everything in nature is connected
- To help children discover that all living things need food, air, water, and shelter to survive
- To help children discover that we depend on the natural world in order to stay alive
- To help children discover that wildlife can be found almost anywhere

• To help children discover that diversity is a necessary and beautiful part of the natural environment

Goal: *To help children develop a sense of appreciation and respect for the integrity of the natural world*
Related Objectives:

• To help children understand that the natural world is ordered, balanced, and harmonious
• To instill in young children a sense of respect for all living and nonliving elements of the natural world

Goal: *To foster in young children a sense of caring for Planet Earth and an understanding that different forms of pollution and misuse harm the natural environment*
Related Objectives:

• To help children understand that Earth is our home
• To help children appreciate the need to relate to the natural world in a respectful, caring way
• To help children recognize different types of pollution (noise pollution, visual pollution, air pollution, water pollution, etc.)
• To help children understand that pollution is harmful to people and the natural environment

Goal: *To help children understand that they are a part of the natural world, not separate from it*
Related Objectives:

• To help children understand that the health and well-being of people and the quality of their life are affected by what happens to the natural environment
• To help children understand that the actions of individuals and groups of people affect other individuals, society, and the natural environment

Goal: *To give young children ideas on how they can contribute to the well-being of Planet Earth*
Related Objectives:

• To involve children in simple pollution prevention activities (recycling, proper disposal of trash, etc.)
• To involve children in simple conservation activities (e.g., using only small amounts of water, paper, etc., or using only as much as they need)
• To help young children learn how they can live lightly on Planet Earth (e.g., by respecting habitats, not picking wildflowers, etc.)

Quality Indicators

A quality early childhood environmental education program must reflect "best practices" in both early childhood education and environmental education. Three quality indicators reflecting best practices common to both early childhood education and environmental education are outlined below, along with a brief discussion of each. These quality indicators are based on the "principles" outlined by Cohen (1992) in a review of the literature on children and ecology and are consistent with what is known about how young children learn.

1. Active versus passive learning opportunities. Young children learn by doing, that is, by being actively involved with people and objects in their environment. Young children construct their own systems of knowledge, and can do so only when given opportunities for both physical and mental engagement with the world around them (Bredekamp, 1987; Piaget, 1962). Quality early childhood programs are built around this understanding of how young children learn and are characterized by active exploration on the part of the child (Cohen & Trostle, 1990).

The environmental education literature supports a similar hands-on and experiential approach to learning (Burrus-Bammel & Bammel, 1990; Hart, 1981; Iozzi, 1989). Environmental educators are encouraged to engage the senses and involve the basic domains of learning—cognitive, affective, and psychomotor (Burrus-Bammel & Bammel, 1990).

2. Direct versus abstract experiences with nature and natural systems. Quality early childhood programs are based on the knowledge that young children learn more from what is real and concrete than what is abstract or representational (Bredekamp, 1987). Environmental education also advocates a direct versus abstract learning approach (Burrus-Bammel & Bammel, 1990; Cornell, 1979; Council on Outdoor Education, 1989; Kellert, 1985; Nichols, 1989; Tanner, 1980). Quality programs in early childhood environmental education, then, provide opportunities for direct experiences with nature and natural materials such as twigs, soil, mud, stones, leaves, and grass (Dighe,1993).

3. Balance of teacher-initiated and child-initiated explorations. While quality early childhood education programs encourage child-initiated explorations, they also recognize the importance of the teacher's role in introducing and facilitating learning activities (Bredekamp, 1987). The environmental education literature advocates a similar balance of teacher-initiated and child-initiated explorations (Knapp, 1983; Long, 1986; Peterson & Hungerford, 1981), as does the literature specifically addressing environmental education with young

children (Dighe, 1993; Furman, 1990; Klein, 1991; Wilson, 1993b).

Curricular Implications

Based on the research foundations for early childhood environmental education and the three quality indicators presented above, a set of 12 curricular implications or guidelines have been developed. Following is a listing of these implications along with suggested program applications.

1. Infuse environmental education into all aspects of the early childhood curriculum.

Clearly specified in the environmental education literature is the importance of an interdisciplinary approach versus "a subject apart" approach (Burrus-Bammel & Bammel, 1990; Buethe & Smallwood, 1987; Caduto, 1984/85; Ham, Rellergert-Taylor, & Krumpe, 1987/88). Such an orientation also matches the approach advocated for early childhood education, where best practices call for an integrated curriculum versus a subject-by-subject approach to education (Bredekamp, 1987).

Program applications:

- Introduce elements of the natural world (shells, stones, dried grasses and leaves, plants, animals, sand, water, twigs, etc.) into the physical environment of the classroom. Choose materials that foster an appreciation of the beauty and diversity of the natural world and that can be used for observation, decoration, and/or manipulation.
- Provide books, posters, and other materials (e.g., music, photographs, etc.) that portray the natural world as beautiful and worthy of respect.
- Plan nature-related activities in the areas of art, music, dance, dramatic play, and all other aspects of the curriculum.

2. *Value play as the most appropriate learning medium for young children.*

Whether learning about the natural environment or any other area of understanding, young children learn best when they are having fun. Play is the child's work and respects their intrinsic motivation to learn. Play also facilitates the integration of learning across all developmental domains (cognitive, language, affective, social, physical, etc.) and encourages children to learn by way of exploration and discovery (Bredekamp, 1987).

Program applications:

- Devote extended periods of time (approximately 45-60 minutes during a half-day program) to child-selected play activities.

- Provide a variety of materials that encourage differing types and levels of play (from simple manipulative items to props for dramatic play). To help children learn about nature, include materials and props relating to the natural world (e.g., animal figurines, puzzles with nature-related themes, animal costumes and puppets, child-sized gardening tools, magnifiers, rubber stamps with nature-related figures, simple camping equipment, materials from the outdoors, etc.).

- Encourage and extend children's play by making comments and suggestions, asking questions, and serving as a play partner. Focus comments, suggestions, and questions on the child's interests and activities. Respect the child's agenda or plan when entering his or her play activity.

- Provide frequent opportunities for exploration and experimentation in a variety of outdoor settings (e.g., digging in the dirt, observing insects and other types of wildlife, hiking through a wooded area,

skating on ice, raking leaves, collecting pebbles or shells, climbing over logs, etc.).

3. *Facilitate the child's physical, mental, and emotional engagement with the natural environment.*

Young children learn by being actively involved with materials, peers, and adults (Bredekamp, 1987; Piaget, 1962). Effective learning, however, requires more than physical involvement. Mental and emotional engagement are also required. Following are some examples of how to facilitate engagement in the physical, mental, and emotional domains.

Program applications for promoting physical engagement:

- Provide opportunities for hands-on manipulation of real (versus representational) objects. For example, a hands-on manipulation of leaves could include raking leaves, carrying leaves to the compost pile, making leaf rubbings, and floating leaves in water. A representational activity, on the other hand, might be to color in a line drawing of a leaf. If representational materials are used, they should always be paired with the real items that they represent.

- Arrange the environment to accommodate different types of physical activity (from working with small manipulative items such as puzzle pieces or art materials, to large muscle involvement with such things as rakes, shovels, logs to climb on, etc.).

- Provide opportunities for rich sensory experiences through what can be seen, felt, tasted, smelled, and heard.

- Provide materials that are manipulable, concrete, and promote children's physical interaction with them.

- Provide firsthand experiences with objects, people, and events in a variety of situations.

Program applications for promoting mental engagement:

- Provide materials and activities that relate to the children's interests. This will motivate them to experiment and explore.
- Allow children to make choices as to what materials to use and how to use them. Making choices involves cognitive engagement.
- In choosing learning materials and planning experiences, consider both familiarity and novelty. In learning new concepts and ideas, young children need a cognitive link to what is already familiar to them. Yet, to maintain interest and to move to new levels of understanding, novelty of experience is also important. A healthy balance between familiar and unfamiliar materials and experiences provides the best learning situations for young children.
- Encourage children to think critically and creatively. The use of thought-provoking questions versus minimal-response questions is a good technique to use. Examples of thought-provoking questions include "What would happen if we brought this snow inside?" and "What do you think we might find under this log?" Examples of minimal-response questions, on the other hand, include "What color is this leaf?" and "What was the first thing we found by the tree?"
- Introduce materials with varying degrees of complexity. This will help children manipulate the materials both physically and cognitively.
- Introduce open-ended activities in which children have the opportunity to do some of the thinking and planning.

- Encourage children to analyze cause-and-effect situations.
- Emphasize the thinking process rather than the product.

Program applications for promoting emotional engagement:

- Establish an environment in which feelings of fun, excitement, and success are the norm.
- Provide opportunities for children to bring about changes in their environment (e.g., digging holes in the ground, raking leaves, planting flowers, rolling logs, etc.). Opportunities for impacting the environment set the stage for intrinsic motivation and feelings of success.
- Recognize and praise unique thoughts, ideas, and contributions.
- Encourage children to express their ideas and feelings through a variety of modes (written and spoken words, arts, crafts, dramatic play, etc.).

4. *Focus on conceptual, rather than rote, learning.*

Children learn by constructing their own knowledge about the world, not by memorizing facts. Rote learning tends to focus on isolated bits of information. Conceptual learning, on the other hand, tends to focus on meaningful understandings.

Program applications:

- Emphasize experiencing versus teaching.
- Emphasize qualities and characteristics versus labels (i.e., the names of things). (The use of labels is fine, if this is not emphasized over attention to qualities and characteristics and if it results from child-initiated learning.)
- Engage the children in interactive discussion versus having them listen to facts.
- Encourage active exploration, experimentation, and problem solving.

5. *Attend to the message as well as the activities and materials.*

Curriculum for young children is sometimes defined as everything they experience and thus includes the physical environment, the daily routine, and the way people interact with each other and the rest of the natural environment. Every aspect of an early childhood program sends some type of message to the children. To foster positive attitudes toward the natural environment or about oneself, related positive messages must be sent (Wilson, 1993a).

Program applications:
- Establish a classroom environment that is warm, nurturing, and safe.
- Use items from nature to decorate the classroom, thus helping students recognize the beauty of nature.
- Provide a variety of natural materials (plant/animal life, water, etc.) for children to explore, thus fostering an appreciation of the diversity and wonder inherent in nature.
- Choose children's books with positive messages about the natural environment. Avoid books that present elements of nature as mean or bad (e.g, The Three Little Pigs, in which "the big bad wolf will huff and puff and blow your house down"; or Little Red Riding Hood, in which the big bad wolf wants to eat your grandmother).
- Display children's nature-related art projects.

6. *Provide daily opportunities for positive interactions with different natural materials (plants, animals, water, soil, etc.).*

Children need frequent positive experiences with the natural world if they are to develop feelings of caring and respect for it (Carson, 1956; Harvey, 1989/90; Peterson & Hungerford, 1981).

Program applications:
- Provide both indoor and outdoor nature-related experiences on a daily basis.
- Encourage children to use objects from nature for their creative expression activities (art, poetry, dance, etc.).
- Introduce variety and interest in the outdoor environment.
- Invite wildlife to the outdoor learning area by establishing suitable habitats.
- Introduce plants and animals into the classroom.
- Provide a variety of nature-related field experiences (through nature walks, visits to zoos, nature centers, etc.).
- Arrange opportunities for children to observe and interact with artists, poets, musicians, and others whose work reflects an appreciation for nature and who enjoy sharing their speciality with young children.

7. *Provide the time and place outdoors for safe, pleasant, memorable experiences.*

The amount of time young children spend outdoors is rapidly decreasing. This is due in part to our increasingly technological way of living and the fact that more and more children are growing up in urban areas, where there are fewer opportunities for direct contact with the natural world (Burrus-Bammel & Bammel, 1990; Cohen & Horm-Wingerd, 1993). Yet, unless children spend time outdoors, they are at risk of never developing an understanding and appreciation of the natural environment (Callander & Power, 1992; Peterson & Hungerford, 1981; Wilson, 1993a; Wilson, 1993b).

Program applications:
- Encourage exploration of the outdoor environment in a variety of different settings (e.g., wooded areas, meadows, farmland, beaches, etc.).

- Provide outdoor learning environments where children are free to explore and experiment.
- Provide outdoor learning environments that are safe (i.e., free of hazards and with ample space for moving about freely).
- Introduce children to outdoor settings that are rich in natural diversity (i.e., having different types of plants, terrain, soil, rocks, wildlife, etc.).
- Plan the daily routine to allow for children's engagement with the natural environment over an uninterrupted block of time. With careful planning, this can be accomplished even in urban areas with limited access to natural environments. Natural environments may include a nook behind the door where spiders build their webs, a sunken area of the playground where puddles form after a rain, a crack in the sidewalk where ants come and go, and an area of the yard where children are free to dig. Natural environments can also be arranged by adding a variety of free or inexpensive materials. Old tires can be filled with soil and used for planting flowers or potatoes. A pile of rocks can be placed under a tree or near the sandbox. Pine cones, twigs, dried grasses, and leaves can be gathered and placed in buckets for the children to carry around, dump, or bury. Simple things like magnifiying glasses, small spray bottles filled with water, and tools for digging can all encourage engagement with the natural environment.

8. *Promote social interaction and cooperation.*

Everything in the natural world (including humans) is connected. Promoting social interaction and a sense of cooperation can help children experience the meaning and importance of interconnectedness.

Program applications:
- Suggest and model positive social interactions.
- Provide materials and activities that promote adult-child and child-child interaction (e.g., puppets, dramatic play, adult-child cooperative activities such as cooking or gardening).
- Use an interactive versus a "teacher-directed" instructional style.
- Modify the environment, if necessary, so that all children can interact. This may mean offering alternatives to speech (e.g., gestures or sign language) and adaptive equipment for children with disabilities.
- Reinforce positive child-child interaction through recognition and praise (e.g., "Jim and Tina are working together on their art project. I like the way they're sharing the paint.").
- Assist children in solving their own social conflicts (e.g., "Maybe you could tell Jodi that you weren't finished with the magnifying glass.").
- Establish a noncompetitive/cooperative environment. Cooperation can be fostered by adult verbal statements and by activities that need more than one child to accomplish (e.g., having one child hold the paper while another child does the tree rubbing). Situations can also be planned in which negotiation about and cooperation toward a common goal are required (e.g., size, weight, or complexity of materials that requires involvement of more than one child).
- Model cooperative behaviors with colleagues and children.
- Coach children on how to cooperatively plan and negotiate (e.g., "Maybe we could ask Kevin if he has any ideas on how to fix the handle.")

- Foster a sense of community through group planning, negotiating, and discussing.
- Demonstrate an appreciation of diversity of <u>all</u> children (including diversity in the areas of gender, age, culture, ability, socioeconomic status, race, etc.).
- Encourage joint cooperative exploration, experimentation, and problem solving.

9. Provide sufficient adult modeling, guiding, and facilitating.

Adults play a critical role in the early childhood program. It's a role that requires active engagement through close observation and moment-to-moment decision making. Decisions have to be made about when to pose a question or refrain from questioning, when to make comments or offer suggestions or when to allow the child exploration to continue on its own. In introducing young children to the world of nature, the "complete" teacher realizes that he or she must be "an interpreter of the printed word as well as the real world around us" (VandenHazel, 1987/88, p. 25). The "complete" teacher realizes that a good learning environment is one in which both the teacher and the child are initiators in structuring the learning situation, and that there needs to be a healthy balance between teacher-initiated and child-initiated activities.

<u>Program applications:</u>

- Model divergent thinking, critical thinking, curiosity, creativity, and problem solving.
- Be conversant with the children, focusing on their interests and activities.
- Give positive, but accurate, feedback to children's questions and comments.
- Let children know that you respect and value their ideas.

- Use verbal statements that express an appreciation of the natural world.

10. Involve families in the environmental education program.

Early childhood education has long recognized the value of family involvement, with benefits to the child, the parents, and the program. Family involvement can take many different forms, but must always respect the diversity of families.

<u>Program applications:</u>

- Invite families to participate in special nature-related activities at the school (e.g., planting a garden, celebrating Earth Day or the first day of spring, painting with feathers and evergreen sprigs, etc.).
- Invite families to participate in field trips.
- Ask parents to donate recyclable materials such as cardboard boxes, plastic yogurt containers, 2-liter plastic bottles, etc.
- Invite parents to share information about their culture, special interests, and occupations.
- Take advantage of the parents' special knowledge and skills by incorporating what they have to offer into the curriculum.
- Share information with parents on nature-related activities and outings they might do with their children at home or in the community.
- Invite parents to submit <u>their</u> ideas on what nature-related activities and outings might be done with the children at school or in the community.

11. Introduce multicultural perspectives.

Both the natural environment and the human community display great beauty and diversity. These qualities aren't always recognized and appreciated. Early childhood environmental education presented from multicultural perspectives has the potential for enhancing awareness and appreciation of both the natural environment and the human community.

Program applications:

- Introduce nature-related games, songs, and stories from a variety of cultures, especially cultures represented by children in the group.
- Provide opportunities for children to make and/or use materials reflecting a variety of cultures (e.g., musical instruments, mosaics, costumes, etc.).
- Develop an understanding of families' cultural relationships to the environment. Incorporate this understanding into the curriculum, especially by having the parents share activities, stories, etc.

12. *Adapt the physical environment and the curriculum to accommodate children with special needs.*

Young children with special needs should be integrated into typical early childhood environments versus being educated apart from their peers (Safford, 1989; Strain, 1988).

Program applications:

- Provide materials that can be used successfully and satisfactorily by children with varying abilities.
- Provide multimodal learning activities (i.e., activities that allow for more than one way to participate), so that children with a disability or weakness in one area (e.g., hearing, seeing, walking, etc.) can participate in and benefit from the activity through an alternate mode.
- Choose activities and materials that reflect the common interest of young children as well as the specific interests of individual children.

- Model cooperative endeavors and inclusion of less socially skilled children as well as children with disabilities.
- Coach children who need help with social interaction strategies.
- Be sensitive and responsive to individual children's cues and emotional, cultural, linguistic, and developmental needs.
- Focus on abilities versus disabilities.
- Demonstrate an appreciation for diversity in the natural world and the human community.

Conclusions

While the delineation of a rationale and quality indicators for environmental education at the early childhood level represents an important step in developing quality early childhood environmental education programs, such a delineation alone will be insufficient for the task. Also needed is preservice and in-service training focusing specifically on environmental education for preschool children. This training should target both environmental education specialists and early childhood education teachers. Environmental education specialists need information and training on how to work with young children. They need to learn about the unique characteristics of preschool children, the ways in which young children learn, and strategies they can use to engage young children in meaningful learning activities. Early childhood education teachers, on the other hand, need information and training on how and why to incorporate environmental education into their programs. They need an awareness and appreciation of the natural environment as a system to which we all belong. They need to recognize the beauty and mystery inherent in the natural environment and develop an enthusiasm for sharing this with young children.

If environmental education specialists do not have an understanding and appreciation of the early childhood years, they may overlook the importance of including young children in their educational programs or providing programs that are appropriate and meaningful for young children. If early childhood education teachers do not have an appreciation of what environmental education is all about or if they feel that they do not know enough about the natural environment, they may not be open to the idea of making environmental education an important part of their programs. Thus, preservice and in-service training opportunities focusing on early childhood environmental education should be made available to both environmental education specialists and early childhood education teachers. The environmental education literature clearly indicates that the inadequacy of trained teachers and personnel is one of the major barriers to environmental education (Williams, 1992).

References

Braus, J. A., & Wood, D. (1993). Environmental education in the schools—Creating a program that works. Washington, DC: Peace Corps Information Collection and Exchange.

Bredekamp, S. (Ed.). (1987). Developmentally appropriate practice in early childhood programs servicing children from birth through age eight. Washington, DC: National Association for the Education of Young Children.

Buethe, C., & Smallwood, J. (1987). Teachers' environmental literacy: Check and recheck, 1975 and 1985. Journal of Environmental Education, 18 (3), 39-42.

Burrus-Bammel, L. L., & Bammel, G. (1990). Outdoor/Environmental education—An overview for the wise use of leisure. Journal of Physical Education, Recreation, and Dance, 61 (4), 49-54.

Caduto, M. J. (1984/85). A teacher training model and educational guidelines for environmental values education. Journal of Environmental Education, 16 (2), 30-34.

Callander, G. D., & Power, S. (1992). The importance of and opportunities for wildlife in an urban environment. Environmental Education and Information, 11 (3), 173-80.

Carson, R. (1956). The sense of wonder. New York: Harper & Row.

Cohen, S. (1992). Research on children and ecology. Childhood Education, 68 (5), 260.

Cohen, S., & Horm-Wingerd, D. (1993). Ecological awareness among preschool children. Environment and Behavior, 25 (1), 103-20.

Cohen, S., & Trostle, S. L. (1990). This land is our land: Promoting ecological awareness in young children. Childhood Education, 66 (5), 304-10.

Cole, E. (1992). Art and learning. Childhood Education, 68 (5), 285-89.

Cornell, J. B. (1979). Sharing nature with children. Nevada City, CA: Ananda Publications.

Council on Outdoor Education (1989). Outdoor education—Definition and philosophy. Journal of Physical Education, Recreation, and Dance, 60 (2), 31-34.

Dighe, J. (1993). Children and the earth. Young Children, 48 (3), 58-63.

Furman, E. (1990). Plant a potato—Learn about life (and death). Young Children, 46 (1), 15-20.

Ham, S. H.; Rellergert-Taylor, M. H.; & Krumpe, E.E. (1987/88). Reducing barriers to environmental education. Journal of Environmental Education, 19 (2), 25-33.

Hanselman, D.; Raghunathan, M.; & Sarabiihai, K. (1990). Essential learnings in environmental education. Troy, OH: North American Association for Environmental Education.

Harlan, J. (1988). Science experiences for the early childhood years. New York: Merrill Publishing.

Hart, E. P. (1981). Identification of key characteristics of environmental education. Journal of Environmental Education, 13 (1), 12-16.

Harvey, J. R. (1989/90). The relationship between children's experiences with vegetation on school grounds and their environmental attitudes. Journal of Environmental Education, 21 (2), 9-15.

Hayden, H.; Oltman, M.; Thompson-Tucker, R.; & Wood, S. (1987). Avoiding infusion confusion: A practical handbook for infusing environmental activities into your classroom. Amherst Junction, WI: Central Wisconsin Environmental Station.

Henderson, K. A. (1990). Deep ecology and outdoor recreation—Incompatible? Journal of Physical Education, Recreation, and Dance, 61 (3), 77-80.

Iozzi, L.A. (1989). Environmental education and the affective domain. Journal of Environmental Education, 20 (4), 6-13.

James, A. (1992). Will it hurt "shade"? Childhood Education, 68 (5), 262.

Kellert, S. R. (1985). Attitudes toward animals: Age-related development among children. Journal of Environmental Education, 16 (3), 29-39.

Kirkby, M. (1989). Nature as refuge in children's environments. Children's Environments Quarterly, 6 (1), 7-12.

Klein, A. (1991). All about ants: Discovery learning in the primary grades. Young Children, 46 (5), 23-27.

Knapp, C. E. (1983). A curriculum model for environmental values education. Journal of Environmental Education, 14 (3), 22-26.

Lind, K. (1991). Exploring science in early childhood: A developmental approach. Albany, NY: Delmar Publishers.

Long, F. O. (1986). The role of the outdoors in the development of a positive self-concept. Counseling and Human Development, 18 (5), 1-8.

Minnesota Department of Education. (1991). Model learner outcomes for environmental education. St. Paul, MN: Minnesota Department of Education.

Nichols, D. R. (1989). Enhancing learning in the outdoors. Journal of Physical Education, Recreation, and Dance, 60 (2),44-46.

Peterson, N. J., & Hungerford, H. R. (1981). Developmental variables affecting environmental sensitivity in professional environmental educators. In A. B.Sacks, L. A.Iozzi, J. M.Schultz, & R.W ilke (Eds.), Current issues in environmental education and environmental studies (Vol. 7). Columbus, OH: ERIC.

Piaget, J. (1962). Play, dreams, and imitation in children. New York: Norton.

Rejeski, D. W. (1982). Children look at nature: Environmental perception and education. Journal of Environmental Education, 13 (4), 27-40.

Safford, P. L. (1989). Integrating teaching in early childhood: Starting in the mainstream. White Plains, NY: Longman.

Singer, J. Y. (1992). People, parks, and rainforests. Childhood Education, 68 (5), 271.

Strain, P. (1988). LRE for preschool children with handicaps: What we know, what we should be doing. Pittsburg, PA: Western Psychiatric Institute and Clinic.

Tanner, T. (1980). Significant life experiences: A new research area in environmental education. Journal of Environmental Education, 11 (4), 20-24.

VandenHazel, B. J. (1987/88). Teachers as interpreters. Journal of Outdoor Education, 22, 87-88.

Williams, R. (1992). Environmental education and teacher education—Learning for change and participation? In S. R. Sterling (Ed.), Annual Review of Environmental Education. Reading, United Kingdom: Council for Environmental Education, pp. 34-37.

Wilson, R. A. (1993a). Educators for Earth: A guide for early childhood instruction. Journal of Environmental Education, 24 (2), 15-21.

Wilson, R. A. (1993b). Fostering a sense of wonder during the early childhood years. Columbus, OH: Greyden Press.

Wilson, R. A. (1994). Early childhood environmental education programs. (Unpublished data). Bowling Green, OH: Bowling Green State University.

Framework for Quality

Three basic principles:
1. Active vs. passive learning opportunities
2. Direct vs. abstract experiences with nature and natural systems
3. Balance of teacher-directed and child-initiated explorations

Twelve curricular guidelines:
1. Infuse environmental education into all aspects of the early childhood curriculum.
2. Value play as the most appropriate learning medium for young children.
3. Facilitate the child's physical, mental, and emotional engagement with the natural environment.
4. Focus on conceptual, rather than rote, learning.
5. Attend to the message as well as the activities and materials.
6. Provide daily opportunities for positive interactions with different natural materials (plants, animals, water, soil, etc.).
7. Provide the time and place outdoors for safe, pleasant, memorable experiences.
8. Promote social interaction and cooperation.
9. Provide sufficient adult modeling, guiding, and facilitating.
10. Involve families in the environmental education program.
11. Introduce multicultural perspectives.
12. Adapt the physical environment and the curriculum to accommodate children with special needs.

Provide daily opportunities for positive interactions with natural materials.

A Teacher's Story*
Marina Williford

Consternation and anxiety were my first reactions when I heard that the school's playground was not going to be available for our summer school program due to construction of an addition to the building. Without access to the playground, our outdoor activities were going to be limited to one grassy area with nothing but a few trees. I was concerned that there would not be enough for the children to do outside. However, from the first day, the children took over the outdoor agenda and found many interesting things to do.

We went outside every day, and the children always found something new. They picked "flowers" (mostly grasses and weeds) of all colors and sizes. They put them in water, took them home for their mommies, made vases, painted with them, made flower gardens and collages, compared who had the same, the tallest, the most, etc.

Once-made play boundaries were soon expanded, as the children found the trees fascinating. They discovered two bird's nests, which they watched from the building stage to the day the baby birds hatched. They used trees for swinging from, for shade to read a book, or as secret hideouts. They used grass and twigs to make campfires for their "camping" games. They caught different types of bugs that were brought inside and put in bug jars to watch and learn about and then release.

The rain was the most exciting of all! While I thought that the rain would ruin the outdoor time, the children found it fascinating! We watched the grass grow fast and tall and learned why. We made pictures of thunder storms and tornadoes, using tempera paint, shaving cream, water, etc. One child even figured out how to make the color gray. We made rainstorms during circle time and talked about our fear of storms.

We changed our schedule to go outside as often as possible. We took walks. We had an outdoor concert, with everyone playing some type of musical instrument. We observed what the construction workers were doing each day and then made our own building with wood scraps and paint. We took toy trucks and bulldozers in our sandboxes so that we could be construction workers.

The children began to help carry out and set up their own play equipment each day. We made our own lunches and had picnics under the trees. We sang songs, read books, and listened to flannel board stories about bugs and rain and flowers and birds. The children and the adults enjoyed the spontaneous planning and the joy of being outdoors!

---

* Reprinted with permission from the <u>Earthworm</u> newsletter, 1993, Vol. 1, No.1, p. 7.

Accommodate Children with Special Needs

Hope School's Summer Camp Program
Jann Frisk

Who would think of overnight camping with a group of four- and five-year-old children with disabilities? Hope School in Henry County, Ohio, has been doing it for years and highly recommends it! Hope School is operated by the Henry County Board of Developmental Disabilities and offers an early childhood education program to over 100 preschool children during the academic school year. Every summer, the program offers two different types of outdoor experiences for about 40 of their preschool children.

The first type of outdoor experience (Camp 1) lasts three days and two nights and involves four- and five-year-old children. For this camping experience, the young group of campers (usually about 12 children), along with their "teachers," go to a recreational campground to participate in a variety of outdoor activities. They sleep in tents, go swimming, ride horses, make arts and crafts, go on field trips, sing songs around the campfire, do some fishing, play group games, and help with cooking.

The second type of outdoor experience (Day Camp) extends over a four-day period and serves children two through five years of age. Day Camp activities are held at nearby community parks, where children have the opportunity to freely explore, participate in guided nature walks, look for rocks, watch a variety of birds and other wild animals, paint with branches found on the ground, plant seeds, play outdoor games, and sing camp songs. There are usually about 30 children who participate in the Day Camp experience.

The summer camp program was designed to provide quality camp experiences individualized to each person's needs to Henry County citizens who have developmental disabilities and to promote a greater degree of independence for each person. The camp program, while originally developed to serve only persons with disabilities, is now open to typically developing preschoolers as well as children with special needs.

The Hope School Summer Camp Programs are presently being funded through the Henry County Association for Retarded Citizens (HARC), United Way, Hope School's Annual Chicken barbecue, Hope School's popcorn booth open during the Henry County Fair, and camp fees. The campers are asked to pay fees of about $15 to $20, but no one is denied the camping experience because of their inability to pay.

The Hope School Summer Camp Programs serve as a fun-filled vehicle for bringing the world of nature and the world of children together. Throughout the process, multiple goals are accomplished. Young children are given the opportunity to experience an extended period of time in the out-of-doors—an opportunity that would be unavailable to many of them if it weren't for the Hope School program. Through this experience young children come to know the natural world as a safe, pleasant, and fun place to be. They're also introduced to the understanding that the world of nature is full of beauty and mystery, and that it warrants a great deal of respect. The camping activities in which the children participate tend to foster a sense of independence and well-being. They also encourage the growth of friendships and positive self-esteem. While these results are important for all young children, they can be especially critical to young children with disabilities.

Steps and Guidelines for Program Planning
Marcie Oltman

Section Overview

This section outlines steps and guidelines for developing early childhood programs in environmental education settings and provides a rationale for doing so. It was developed by Marcie Oltman, an environmental educator who has worked in a variety of programs for preschool children.

The Early Childhood Opportunity

Early in the last decade a survey was conducted of professional staff and chapter officers in national environmental organizations like the Sierra Club and the National Audubon Society. Thomas Tanner, author of the study, sought to identify the source of these people's environmentally oriented values and, ultimately, why they chose careers based on those values. Most of them cited frequent positive childhood experiences in the outdoors and the encouragement of someone they loved or admired as having the greatest influence on their values and choices (Tanner, 1980). Tanner's study was based on the premise that "significant life experiences" play a major role in determining an individual's adult orientation.

Tanner's study validated what most environmental educators already believed—that, in his words, "children must first learn to love the natural world before they can become profoundly concerned with maintaining its integrity" (p.23). Love of nature is the foundation on which to build future knowledge, attitudes, and skills

as these relate to the natural world. Unfortunately, frequent exposure to the outdoors is now the exception rather than the rule for a rapidly growing population. Instead of focusing on increasing knowledge and skills, environmental educators must often take on the monumental, retroactive task of transforming attitudes as a prerequisite to changing behavior.

In addressing this issue, Tanner (1980), Wilson (1993), and others suggest that early childhood is the ideal time to engage children in the exploration of the natural world. Young children are active learners, using all of their senses and eagerly absorbing information about their environment. RachelCarson said it best in The Sense of Wonder (1956):

> *I sincerely believe that for the child, and for the parent seeking to guide him, it's not half so important to know as to feel. If facts are the seeds that later produce knowledge and wisdom, then the emotions and the impressions of the senses are the fertile soil in which the seeds must grow. The years of early childhood are the time to prepare the soil.* (p. 45)

Although this "get 'em when they're young" philosophy is generally accepted and encouraged, there has been a reluctance in the field of environmental education to seriously consider the preschool audience as legitimate subjects for environmental education programming. Through choice or necessity, environmental education initiatives have concentrated largely on the traditional K-12 population, both in the formal (public and private school systems) and nonformal (nature centers, zoos, museums, etc.) educational settings. However, as most nature centers, zoos, and science museums can attest, there is an ever-increasing demand to provide programs for preschoolers.

There are approximately 10 million children in the United States who are enrolled in some form of child care or preschool program. It would be a mistake to wait until these children enter elementary school before introducing them to environmental education opportunities. Environmental educators need to seriously consider the early stages in a child's development as worthy of their time and attention.

In addition, there is a growing movement to integrate child care into existing school systems, both with formal preschools and informal "latchkey" programs. Therefore, more and more preschool programs will be formally structured within the K-12 system, as is already the case in many school districts across the country. The result is an unprecedented opportunity for the growth of environmental education at the early childhood level. As the audience is ready, willing, and able, environmental educators would do well to offer quality instruction and programming at the early childhood level.

Guidelines for Program Development

Current trends in early childhood programming and the concomitant implications for environmental education suggest the need to develop practical guidelines for designing quality preschool programs in the nonformal sector. Environmental educators, naturalists, interpreters, and other environmental professionals can look to the field of early childhood education for guidance when planning these programs.

Preschoolers are not alien beings, but capable and enthusiastic participants—given the right combination of age-appropriate activities and techniques. Preschool children have a unique set of physical, cognitive, social, and emotional attributes that set them apart from any other age group. Far from limitations, these attributes give the environmental educator a special opportunity to combine a knowledge of child development with appropriate interpretive techniques in a program that both child and educator can enjoy.

The value of early childhood education to the profession of environmental education and nature education is effectively described in <u>Fostering a Sense of Wonder during the Early Childhood Years</u> (Wilson, 1993).

> *Early childhood education uses a child-centered, versus teacher-directed, approach. Early childhood educators realize that young children learn best in an atmosphere that allows freedom of choice and movement, spontaneous initiation of activities, and informal conversations. . . . A child-centered approach is ideal for learning about the natural world. Children do not need direct instruction on how to feel, see, and hear the world around them. Nor is there just one right way to experiment with stones, sticks, and water. Children learn best from their early investigations and experiments in the out-of-doors—or with materials gathered from the out-of-doors—when their activities are guided by interest and curiosity, not by prescribed methods of inquiry.* (pp.9-10)

Over the past few years, the early childhood community has articulated guidelines for early childhood education in the form of "developmentally appropriate practices" (Bredekamp, 1987). These guidelines are based on the work of Piaget, Montessori, Erikson, and others, which recognizes that young children learn by doing. According to a position statement of the National Association for the Education of Young Children (NAEYC):

> *Developmentally appropriate teaching strategies are based on knowledge of how young children learn . . . . The degree to which both teaching strategies and the curriculum are developmentally appropriate is a major determinant of program quality. Developmentally appropriate programs are both age appropriate and individually appropriate; that is, the program is designed for the age group served and implemented with attention to the needs and differences of the individual children enrolled.* (Bredekamp, 1987, p.53)

The key to successful preschool programming is in choosing developmentally appropriate activities. Climbing on stone walls, listening to a raccoon puppet tell about her home in a dead tree, balancing on a rotten log, hopping like a frog, slithering like a snake, and feeling the smooth skin of a salamander all contribute to a child's development in important ways. Child-initiated, child-directed, teacher-supported play is an essential component of developmentally appropriate practice (Bredekamp, 1987). Indeed, the importance of play in a child's cognitive, physical, emotional, and social development is an integral part in un-derstanding how children learn and how adults can facilitate that learning.

Environmental educators inexperienced with preschool children often are frustrated with the inabilities of young children to share, wait their turn, stand in line, and follow directions. This frustration stems from expecting children to see the world through adult eyes. What some adults want to teach and what children are ready to learn are often completely separate things. For example, during a program about birds a naturalist was discouraged by the lack of attention being paid to the black-capped chickadee perched near the group. Instead, the children were fascinated with the glistening pebbles alongside a nearby stream. Instead of insisting that the group focus on the bird, the naturalist joined the children by the stream. More importantly, she let them discover for themselves what was important about the stream. By listening and watching, she learned as much in the process as they did. She discovered that one of the keys to success in a preschool program is to work from a "child-centered" rather than "teacher-directed" perspective (Castle, 1989).

Developmentally appropriate practices offer guidelines for the development of curriculum for young children. Below are selected guidelines from the NAEYC publication (Bredekamp, 1987) that can serve as goals for designing developmentally appropriate environmental education programs for preschool children. Examples of how to implement the guidelines are also provided.

Provide integrated experiences that meet the children's needs and stimulate learning in all developmental areas—physical, social, emotional, and intellectual. For example, provide a program that has a variety of experiences;

room and time to run, leap, balance, and climb; time to nurture friendships and learn about caring and sharing; a chance for children to discover on their own the beauty of nature; and opportunities to learn about how nature works.

Prepare an environment for children to learn through active exploration and interaction with adults, other children, and materials. Young children need to discover for themselves. For this reason, the traditional nature walk "stop and talk" technique is not rewarding or educational for preschoolers—nor is the lecture format, often described as the "chalk and talk." It's important to prepare spaces both inside and out that encourage freedom of movement, creativity, expression, and exploration.

Allow children to choose from activities the teacher has set up or the children spontaneously initiate. Rather than dictating exactly what and when every child does particular activities, this guideline suggests that children be allowed to choose from a variety of activities preselected by the adult according to what interests the children. Habitat puzzles, wooden blocks, animal puppets, paints, sand or water play, and cooking are all excellent examples of the kind of activities that might be offered.

Provide children with concrete learning activities with materials and people relevant to their own life experiences. Preschoolers cannot be expected to understand concepts about things that are too unfamiliar to them. Themes or units of study should be based on what is familiar to the children. Clouds, leaves, rain, pumpkins, rabbits, and ants are all natural objects that most children can relate to. Once the link with what is familiar is established, then some degree of novelty can be added to the learning situation.

Accept that there is often more than one right answer. Children learn from self-directed problem solving and experimentation. Ask open-ended questions that could have a variety of right answers to encourage imagination, thought, and expression. Facts are not of paramount importance at this age, but discovery and wonder are. "What do you think the animal is doing?" is an example of an open-ended question, while "What is this animal called?" represents a fact-oriented question.

Follow routines that help children keep themselves healthy and safe. Following a predictable routine helps children feel comfortable and recognize limits. For example, young children have little concept of what "We'll go outside in ten minutes" means. However, "We'll go outside after snack" is very understandable if the day follows a particular and consistent pattern.

Provide children with daily opportunities for using large muscles and small muscles, for aesthetic expression and appreciation through art and music, and for learning about outdoor environments where they can express themselves freely and loudly. It is not enough to limit children to an occasional "P.E." (physical education) or art activity simply as a time filler. These important elements must be explored as an integrated part of the program with sufficient time devoted to their enjoyment.

Provide opportunities where children's natural curiosity and desire to make sense of their world are used to motivate them to become involved in learning activities. Plant suggestions but let the children take them where they may! Watching a sowbug roll into a ball may lead anywhere from a discussion of how animals protect themselves to creating a dance of animal movements. Regardless of the kinds of activities children may spontaneously create, we can rest assured that they <u>are</u> learning and growing!

A Practical Approach to Program Design

Careful attention to the planning process greatly enhances any program, especially when considering a new audience. Before designing a preschool program, environmental educators would do well to spend as much time as possible visiting local preschools. Much can be learned by observing the children's activities and interactions, the words and phrases the teachers use, and the daily routine of the class.

Becoming familiar with the nature and characteristics of a quality preschool program will serve one well in designing an environmental education program for young children. The following step-by-step approach to developing quality environmental education programs for preschoolers in a nonformal setting may also be helpful.

1. Identify the target audience.

Several factors involving a specific audience will directly affect the format of the proposed program: What are the demographics of the facility's membership or geographical area? Is there a greater need to provide programs for existing groups, such as day cares, or for individual children and families? Are there sufficient staff and facilities to accommodate large groups with varied enrollment numbers or would it be better to limit attendance? Should parent participation be built into the program, or is there a need for "drop-off" arrangements? Would a long-term program best meet the needs of the community and the goals of the facility? Answering these and other pertinent questions will provide the foundation for quality program design.

2. Decide on program format and logistics.

Should the proposed program offer a one-shot session or a six-week, twice-a-week series? Will it be for the general public or an extension of existing K-12 school offerings? What about a summer camp option for preschoolers? Depending upon the format, the following variables should be considered:

<u>Program Length</u>. Program length should be based on the age of the children and what is feasible for the facility. Many centers mistakenly decide program length based solely on the perceived "short attention span" of the audience. It is a common misconception that, because of limited attention span, preschool children can only tolerate a short program of 20-30 minutes. This misconception only serves to shortchange the audience. While it is true that children can become restless and quickly distracted in programs using inappropriate teaching methods (such as lecturing or closed questioning), such behavior may be due to the fact that their developmental needs go unrecognized or ignored. Providing a number of short, age-appropriate and varied activities serves to maximize the abilities of the participants and minimize the frustrations of the instructor (see #3 for specifics). Therefore, depending on the activities and formats chosen, optimum program length should vary between one to three hours.

<u>Teacher/Child Ratio</u>. There should always be a minimum of two supervising adults with a group of preschool children. Nature center personnel might have one instructor for parent/child classes or organized day care groups, provided that guidelines for child supervision are clearly communicated to accompanying adults. For all programs serving three- to five-year-old children, the ratio should be 2:20 with an optimum of

2:14. For younger children, more adults per children will be required.

Classroom Space. The classroom should have enough space to accommodate a variety of learning centers well equipped with appropriate art, play, and hands-on materials on a temporary or permanent basis. Areas in the classroom might include (a) a projects area with free access to a variety of art materials, (b) a painting easel, (c) "cubbies" for personal belongings, (d) a block and toy area, (e) a dramatic play area, (f) a sand and/or water table, (g) a center for live animals (provided a suitable habitat can be maintained for them), (h) a fine motor area equipped with puzzles and/or other materials requiring fine motor skills, (i) a book area, etc. Classrooms should ideally have easy access to bathrooms, kitchen, a water supply, and the outdoors. Carpeted areas and child-sized table and chairs are also recommended. If planning a long-term program, a child care state licensing agency should be consulted for additional guidelines.

Schedule. Different days of the week and different times of the day (i.e., morning, afternoon, or evening) might be considered. Factors that might affect attendance include nap times or library story hours. Once a schedule is established, it should be followed consistently and regularly.

Registration. For program formats where children are dropped off for any length of time, it is important to have the following information readily available: name and age of the child; name, address, and phone of the parents; emergency names and phone numbers; name of the person picking up the child; any known allergies or medical conditions; and an emergency release form.

3. *Design a predictable program structure that incorporates a variety of learning opportunities.*

Following a predictable, consistent routine will help children feel safe and in control. This will help tremendously in guiding children's behavior. Typical programs should include some or all of the following segments.

Gathering Activities. Designed as a large group activity at the start of a program, "gathering" can establish the topic or theme of the day. It's best to choose activities that are familiar, require little adult guidance, and provide opportunities for creativity: giant murals to paint or color on, playdough sculptures, nature puzzles, puppets, painting with natural objects, etc. Gathering activities provide a comfortable way for latecomers to assimilate into the group.

Self-Directed Learning. During self-directed learning, children are free to explore various activities offered throughout the classroom. This option provides freedom of choice in a controlled yet unstructured environment. Self-directed learning accomplishes a number of objectives—it provides opportunities for active exploration, socialization, decision making, and satisfying natural curiosity. It is especially important in establishing group interaction in a format where individuals register separately. However, it is important for any group, particularly organized school groups, to be given time to explore a new space and become comfortable in new surroundings.

Learning Circle. The learning circle serves as a nature lesson provided that the appropriate teaching techniques are used. It may include a short game, demonstration, or hands-on activity designed to extend the theme of the day. Puppets, magic, mystery, props, costumes, murals, pictures, etc. can be used to structure an activity that addresses a specific but simple, nature-related message. The message should be kept to one single idea. Everyone should have an opportunity to participate, and a hands-on component is a must. For example, if the theme is trees, a learning objective might be for the students to learn about the parts of a tree. The learning activity might be sturctured around a "learning bag" prepared in advance. The learning bag is made by placing one paper lunch bag inside another. Several tree seedlings are separated into parts—leaves, stems, and roots. These parts are placed in the "inside" bag. A whole seedling is placed between the two bags so it cannot be seen. While in a circle, children are invited to discuss what they know about trees. Each child then reaches in the bag and takes out one item. Discussion then focuses on what plant part each child picked, including its physical characteristics, possibly its name and, if possible, what it does for the plant. The whole plant is then pulled out from between the two bags and children are given the opportunity to identify the part they picked earlier.

Art Projects. Art projects can enhance a preschool program in a number of ways: they reinforce the theme, provide valuable opportunities for fine motor skill development, serve as a physical reminder of a special event or idea, and stimulate conversation at home or school. The ideal project is process oriented and open-ended, allowing children to decide for themselves how they want to do it. For example, during spring pond week, dragonflies can be made out of pipe cleaners, Styrofoam disks (used in packing), and tissue paper. Children thread as many disks as they want onto the pipe

cleaner and wrap tissue paper around the middle for wings. Although they may have a model to look at, they should be encouraged to be as creative as they please. Some of the finished products might not look like the model dragonfly at all! That's fine, because **the process is more important than the product.** Providing a variety of materials for art projects and allowing children to make choices about what to make and how to make it help children gain confidence in their artistic and decision-making skills. Recycled materials should be used whenever appropriate. Having shifts (small groups) of 3-4 children working on a project during self-directed learning allows for more individualized help. Art projects should be an optional activity, not mandatory.

Toileting. While children should be aware that they can use the bathroom whenever they need to, it's a good idea to first establish guidelines. Children should always be supervised by an adult. If the program is longer than one hour, a scheduled group bathroom time is recommended. If a child needs to use the toilet during a scheduled activity, asking if others need to go can avoid unnecessary trips. For extended programs, children should have a complete change of clothes in case of an accident.

Outside. Children should spend as much time outside as possible! There should be some unstructured time for running, jumping, climbing, and playing in safe natural areas away from typical playground equipment. While overstructuring activities should be avoided, it may be helpful at times to use focusing techniques and to play simple games. Ideas include going on a hole or home hunt, collecting interesting objects, pretending to be baby spiders floating on gossomer strands, coming up with an original name for an animal that lives in the pond, and running to the opposite end of the field.

Snack. Programs that are two or more hours in length should include an easy nutritional snack with juice. Snack might be offered during story time and, if possible, made with the children earlier in the day. Salamander-shaped cookies, ants on a log (peanut butter and raisins on celery sticks), and granola are perfect snacks!

Story and Songs. Reading or telling a story is an excellent teaching technique for before, during, or after outdoor adventures. Fictional stories that children can relate to with clear illustrations hold their attention best. Choosing a story that relates to the theme is optimal but not always possible or necessary. Books and stories shared with the children should present nature or elements of nature in a positive and realistic light. Songs can be sung throughout the day or during a music and movement time. Songs with simple, repetitive melodies and lots of motion are best.

4. *Design developmentally appropriate themes.*

Each session should have a theme chosen for relevance and age appropriateness. Three-year-olds need very concrete themes that are meaningful to them. These may be seasonally based. Appropriate themes for fall could include leaves, fall colors, pumpkins, and apples. Progress through the seasons with additional themes like snow, winter birds, rain, frogs, etc. Four- and five-year-olds can handle slightly more abstract themes but must still be able to relate to them. For instance, fall harvest, insects, weather, and amphibians are all appropriate for the older preschooler. As a general rule, abstract topics or topics about things not present (and thus not real to the children)—such as the rain forest—are more appropriate for older school-aged children.

Learning to Love the World of Nature

Knowledge about children's lives, loves, challenges, and motivations is invaluable in planning meaningful and pleasurable nature-related experiences. Positive and meaningful experiences with the world of nature broaden young children's base of knowledge about the world around them and enhance their ability to internalize these experiences in a way that is relevant to their level of development. Most of all, the preschool years are about learning to love— ourselves, each other, and the natural environment. With nurturing and encouragement, such a love will last a lifetime.

References

Bredekamp, S. (Ed.) (1987). Developmentally appropriate practice in early childhood programs serving children from birth through age eight. Washington, DC: National Association for the Education of Young Children.

Carson, R. (1956). The sense of wonder. New York: Harper & Row.

Castle, K. (1989, Summer). Child-centered teaching: Through children's eyes. Childhood Education, 65 (4), 209-12.

Tanner, T. (1980). Significant life experiences: A new research area in environmental education. Journal of Environmental Education, 11 (4), 20-24.

Wilson, R. A. (1993). Fostering a sense of wonder during the early childhood years. Columbus, OH: Greyden Press.

Tips, Tricks, and Techniques
Pamela A. Mowbray

> **Section Overview**
> This section provides a variety of guidelines and suggestions for working effectively with preschool children in an environmental education setting. Suggestions provided include ideas on how to manage difficult situations (e.g., transition times, behavioral concerns, etc.) encountered when working with a group of young children. These suggestions are offered by Pamela Mowbray, who has worked both as a naturalist and a preschool teacher.

Overall Guidelines

1. Know what you want the children to learn.
Write it down in one sentence and keep it to one single idea. Don't be surprised, however, if what the children learn is something entirely different than what you planned.

2. Look for self-evident aspects of a theme.
Examples: Birds have feathers, mammals have fur, a frog's skin is wet.

3. Keep in mind the demographics of your group.
If you have preregistration, take down the age of each child. You may also wish to know whether or not the children attend a preschool program, as this may affect their ability to follow directions and work in a group. Plan group activities to meet the needs of the youngest child in the group, especially in terms of games, crafts, concepts, and directions.

4. Relate to children from their reality, through their eyes.
Because young children are ego-centered, it's important to relate new ideas or concepts to things they are already familiar with. Examples: Look at your hands and see that you have five fingers. Look at raccoon tracks and see that their paws have five digits. When we're hungry, we go to our kitchen or refrigerator. When animals are hungry, they look for plants and other foods found in nature.

5. Maintain simplicity in language, concepts, and directions.
Describe and demonstrate activities step by step. Limit games or craft activities to two or three steps for three-year-olds; four or five steps for four- and five-year-olds. Let the children know that they may need to share or take turns and wait for a few minutes, but that they'll each get a turn to do an activity.

6. Plan open-ended activities.
"Open-ended" means that there is no one way in which an activity must be done. In doing arts and crafts, children's products need not look exactly like a model or picture. Children should be free to use their imagination and express their creativity. It's important to accept and affirm children's ideas and perceptions. Have children describe their pictures or projects to you, instead of trying to label or describe it for them. Give children a "five minute notice" before ending an art or craft activity, so that they have time to bring it to closure. In planning the day, however, allot plenty of time for each activity, so that children have the time to do it well.

Tips, Tricks, and Techniques
<u>Tips:</u>

- Greet children and talk to them at their level of sight. Get down on your knees, sit on the floor, and make yourself available to them.

- Have name tags or have the children make their own as an introductory activity. This will give the children a sense of belonging to the group and will allow you to be more personal when you can call them by name. You may wish to have nature-related rubber stamps or stickers available for the children to use in decorating their name tags.

- Consider having "learning centers" or "stations" available for the four- and five-year-old children. (These may offer too many choices and be overwhelming to the three-year-olds.) Learning centers may feature (a) art materials and activities, (b) books or magazines, or (c) sensory materials, such as acorns in a tub, ice and water, rocks, shells, etc.

- Do a variety of storytelling, song, and movement activities. Include sensory, art, and exploratory/discovery activities. Examples: Paint with spray bottles. Cut old sponges into different shapes for sponge painting. Roll beads or marbles through paint in a paper-lined box or box lid. Paint with pine sprigs and other objects from nature. Provide sand, nuts, leaves, pine needles, etc. for rich sensory experiences.

- Develop large butcher paper murals, depicting one continuous story. Read or tell a story and then discuss it with the children. Have them recall images from the story and then draw the images on the paper. Drawing on a large sheet of paper works well if children lie down on the floor to do their drawings. The paper might be divided into different sections to represent different parts of the story (e.g., forest, field, cave, sky, lake, etc.).

- Use small containers and applicators for gluing activities. This will make it easier for the children to use small amounts of glue and to apply it where they want it. Small ketchup cups, old paint brushes, glue sticks, and glue brushes work well. These can be purchased from craft or teacher stores or catalogues.

- Have a tub of warm soapy water on a chair or low table, with paper towels and a waste basket nearby. This will allow children to be independent in washing hands and cleaning up and will also save time.

- Have alternative choices for children who finish an activity while you are still assisting others. Noncompetitive games work well. Examples: tossing pine cones into a box or basket, tossing rings on antlers, or tossing acorns into a turtle shell. (This may be too difficult for three-year-olds, but great fun for four- and five-year-olds.)

<u>Tricks:</u>

- Keep visuals or objects concealed at first to build curiosity and allow for surprise. Items might be brought out in a closed shopping bag, old suitcase, or covered box. Children can try to guess what's in the box or bag.

- After discussing and passing several different objects, cover them with a cloth, remove one (out of sight of the children), and have the children guess which one is missing.

- Change or make up words to a familiar song to fit your theme. Add finger, hand, and body movements.

- Change familiar games (e.g., "Hokey Pokey," "If You're Happy and You Know

It," or "Head, Shoulders, Knees, and Toes") to include the names of animal parts, or tree, flower, or insect names and parts.

- Encourage dramatic play by providing appropriate props. Examples: tissue paper streamers taped to arms for wings; large appliance boxes with cut outs to make hollow trees, caves, or other animal homes. Dramatic play can be open-ended with children making up a "story" as they play, or used for dramatizing a story introduced to the group.
- Have children hunt for partly hidden objects. Make the items easy to find.
- Have children identify objects in "feely" or "smelly" bags.

Techniques:

For Transitions—

- Let children and parents know that you'll be starting a new activity in five minutes. This five-minute notice allows children to finish what they're doing (coloring, playing, etc.) and get ready to begin the program or change from one activity to another.
- Let children know just before one activity is done what they will be doing next (e.g., "We'll take two more turns, then we'll be painting with feathers"). Anticipation of what's coming next can help ease the transition.

For Guiding Behavior—

- Model effective language techniques for children to use with each other. Examples: "I need room to see, please" or "I'm not ready to share yet" or "Will you share that with me when you're done?" Modeling language for children can give them the words or tools to verbalize what they're thinking but may not say out of shyness or lack of the necessary language

skills or understanding of how to express themselves. Helping children use appropriate language is also an effective way to avoid or minimize disputes.

- Put all directions and requests in positive terms. Use more "do's" than "don'ts." Instead of saying "Don't interrupt," you might say "Please look and see." Explain to the children the kinds of behaviors you want to see (e.g., "I like it when you share," "Now it's time to sit still and listen"). Children generally respond to "don't" messages by focusing on the negative behavior. "Don't" messages may also cause children to feel that they're bad. Children aren't bad; they just don't make the right choices all the time.
- Guide children to positive behaviors or alternative activities. This approach gives children a chance to focus on a positive experience versus a problem. Examples: If children are arguing about sharing materials or space, direct them to another activity or area in the room.
- Help children focus on your story or demonstration by saying, "I see your hand is up and I know you have lots of things to share with us about animals, but we'll have time to share later during our craft or hike. Right now, I need you to look and listen."
- Remember: The more age-appropriate the activity, the less guiding behavior will be necessary.

Getting Started Is as Easy as A-B-C
Emily Sedgwick Galvin

Sharing nature with young children is as simple and easy as A-B-C:
    A. Use concrete materials.   B. Provide hands-on activities.   C. Use repetition.

A. CONCRETE MATERIALS. Talking about trees indoors can be confusing to preschool children. Young children need concrete objects to manipulate and investigate with their senses. A picture may be worth a thousand words, but a preschooler loses interest after the third word: "This picture is . . ." Pictures are symbols for the real thing. Yet young children cannot always make the connection between the symbol and what it represents. To learn about a tree, they need a "here and now" tree. Awareness, observation skills, curiosity, and natural relationships will be stimulated when seeds can be seen and felt, or caught falling from the tree, or picked up off the ground. Preserved tree flowers, nuts, or laminated autumn leaves given to students in the classroom will provide a sensory experience, but the object and the tree may have little meaning.

    Nature provides concrete, "here and now" experiences, where changes are constantly occurring. Frequent exploration of the same outdoor area will reveal differences that can be compared to past experiences and allow children to construct their own knowledge through direct observation and manipulation.

B. HANDS-ON ACTIVITIES.

> *I hear and I forget*
> *I see and I remember*
> *I do and I understand.*

    "Doing" involves process skills. Facts are learned and information obtained via process skills. Learning a fact, such as the name of a tree like the white pine, requires many process skills: observing the color and shape of the needlelike leaves, feeling the texture of the leaves and noting that they are held in bundles, smelling crushed leaves, counting leaves in the bundles, and comparing these leaves to the leaves of other trees. As an analogy, a cake is a product resulting from the process skills of sifting, measuring, following a sequence, mixing, adding ingredients, pouring, and baking.

    Handling natural objects and observing their size, color, shape, texture, or weight provides sensory experiences and opportunities to construct knowledge about the natural world. By manipulating objects in a variety of ways, children can learn valuable lessons about how they can affect their environment, and how the natural world can affect them.

    The process of knowing facts or making products must come first. Neither facts nor products have meaning without understanding the process. Developmentally appropriate processes for preschool children are

OBSERVING: Observing with all of the senses.

COMPARING: Using the senses to recognize likenesses and differences.

CLASSIFYING: Sorting and grouping likenesses and differences through observation.

MEASURING: Observing, comparing, and classifying with tools. Tools can be standard metric measuring instruments, or antiquated measuring instruments such as "feet" (the foot size of some person who decided it could be a tool for measuring) or a "yard" (an arm length of perhaps the same rather large adult). The simplest measuring tools are related to body parts and common objects: the hand, a finger, the distance from the ground to the knee, a paper clip (longer than or shorter than) , a cup or half a cup (filling it up or deciding that something is too big to fit in it).

COMMUNICATING: Building language development skills by using the vocabulary that describes objects and processes. Encourage children to express their experiences, thoughts, and feelings verbally. Language is not developed in a vacuum; it must be practised.

C. REPETITION. Repetition is an important key to learning. Concepts need to be presented in different ways, in different places, and at different times.

A tree can be poetic. In response, songs, stories, and fingerplays about trees can be introduced. Trees can be likened to children: skin to bark, arms to branches, trunks to trunks, feet to roots. Trees can be dramatized. They can also be measured—leaves or branches picked up on a nature walk can be compared for longest, fattest, or darkest. Tying a string on a twig in early spring and observing growth provides concrete, observable change and an interesting measurement activity. Apples, oranges, cherries, and nuts can be used for endless cooking activities. Nature cooking can relate to concept development, like making "hideouts" to represent winter hibernation.

> Recipe for "hideouts"
> Mix: 1 cup peanut butter
>   1/2 cup honey
>   3/4 to 1 cup powdered milk
> Form into balls and stick apple pieces, raisins, or date bits into the middle, smoothing over the opening.
> (from <u>Yearful of Circle Times</u> by Liz & Dick Wilmes)

Using the A-B-C Approach

Catching falling leaves is a hands-on, concrete, observable activity demonstrating gravity. That's physics! So is drinking through a straw to represent how a tree takes up water from its roots. Putting a paper flower cutout on top of a cup and sticking a straw through it becomes an insect sucking nectar.

Old World painters wanted to duplicate nature. Impressionist painters attempted to capture the color and light of nature. Modern artists symbolize their impressions and feelings about nature. Young children, too, can creatively express themselves artistically in many different ways. Tempera paint, water colors, a variety of papers in a range of colors and sizes, glue, scissors, markers, crayons, recyclables, and nature treasures can serve as media for art activities.

Using A-B-C makes nature study with young children simple and easy. To get started, just open the door and go explore.

Ideas from CSUF Children's Center
Susan Hopkins and Janice Sheffield

Section Overview

Cal State Fullerton Children's Center serves children ages 6 months to 5 1/2 years and offers an environmentally focused curriculum. This curriculum, based on how children learn best, has become a natural part of daily life in ways in which children, families, and teachers can participate actively together. For example, children help feed the tortoises, bunnies, and birds as part of their morning program. Everyone works to save electricity and water by turning off lights and faucets when not in use. Recycling is sometimes used for fund raising, an activity that involves the families as well as the children. Families are informed about the program's activities through special events and classroom newsletters. The most important aspects of the environmental education program are as follows:

1. The activities are part of daily life—not projects done occasionally.
2. All activities involve direct, active participation by the various members of the community and build upon children's awareness of their world.
3. Families are informed and involved as much as possible.

The following list of activities is typical of many that occur at the Children's Center. These particular activities were developed by Janice Sheffield and used as a part of a Peace Camp—a week-long day camp for children ages 3 1/2 to 7 1/2 years. The purpose was to expose children to concepts and activities relating to the creation of a more peaceful world.

Sample Environmental Education Activities
- Make recycled paper from paper scraps.
- Make litter bags to use in the car. Use a lunch sack and cut a hole in the back so it can be put on a door handle. Reinforce the top of the hole with tape.
- Go on a walk and pick up litter (no glass). Look at the area before and after you clean up. Discuss how it makes you feel to see it each way. How can garbage/trash affect people and animals? Ask children how they think the garbage/trash got on the ground. Take pictures of before and after to share with parents. Read the book Where Does All The Garbage Go? by Melvin Berger.
- Make a collage of people-made trash and nature "trash" (leaves, twigs, dried grass). How do you feel when you look at the people-made trash? nature's trash?

- Learn about water pollution. Put clean clear water in an aquarium and then each day add something to the water (playdough, vegetable oil, string, napkin, etc.). Each day record what the children say about the new addition and the condition of the water. What happened to our clear, clean water? What can we do to help keep our water clean?

- Let water drip into a container to see how much water will collect in just five minutes. Discuss: What if we washed our hands for lunch and left the water running while we were eating? How much water would that be? What happens to the water after it goes down the drain? Is it still clean? Take off the drain pipe and see how clean it is. What could we do with the water we collected for our experiment? (E.g., water the plants.)

- Make signs to remind people to pick up their trash. Talk about how even adults get angry about different issues and how picketing is one way they can use their words to let others know what they do not like.

- Make a plaster cast collection of animal tracks you find. Directions: Vaseline the inside surface of a card strip and form it into a ring. Press the ring into the ground around the animal track. Pour plaster in the form and wait for it to dry.

- Make bark impressions in play dough. Bring playdough back to the classroom and fill with plaster. Compare the different types of bark. How are they the same/different?

- Plant or adopt a tree. Trees help keep the air we breathe fresh and clean. Take pictures of "your" tree throughout the year to see how it changes. Do any insects, birds, and/or animals enjoy the use of the tree? Make leaf and bark rubbings of the tree. Is there anything the class can do to help the tree grow?

- Do a tree study. What is the tallest tree in your area? the widest?

- Collect soil from different areas. Keep it warm and moist in a shallow dish. See what germinates. Compare how the soil is the same/different.

- Study "plant power." Walk and look for plants growing up through the cracks of the sidewalk, street, between rocks, etc.

- Make a worm farm. Feed and care for the worms.

- Experiment with Styrofoam pieces and cornstarch packing pieces. Fill two containers with water. Place the Styrofoam in one and the cornstarch packing pieces in the other. What happens? Which do you think is better for the environment? Keep the experiment going for a few days, so that the children can see that the Styrofoam will not break down from the water.

- Look for the recycling symbol (triangle made up of three arrows) on different items (glass, aluminum, plastic, etc.). Does everything have the symbol?

- Collect materials for recycling (cans, paper, plastic, etc.). Sell what has been collected and use the money to help buy a tree or other materials for the school.

- Have classroom pets. Caring for pets helps strengthen children's understanding of what all animals need. Learn to "listen" to the pet and it will "talk" to you. (Our pet goldfish splashes her tail when she wants to be fed. If everyone is too far away, she will stop swimming around and stay in one place and just look at us.)

- Use washcloths to wipe up spills and clean up after art activities. Wash and use again. How many paper towels does it take to clean up 1/2 cup of spilled water? How many cloth wipes?

Keepers of the Earth
Environmental Awareness for Early Childhood Educators
Dona Greene Bolton

Section Overview

Each summer, Kent State University offers a one-week environmental awareness workshop for early childhood educators. Dona Greene Bolton, who leads this workshop, shares with participants her philosophy and approach to introducing young children to the world of nature. Dona speaks from her own experience as the outdoor education teacher at Kent State University's Child Development Center, where she works with children ages four through six. Following are some of Dona's reflections on this program and her experiences over the years.

Reflecting on and Responding to the Natural Environment

People today spend most of their time in artificial or people-made environments. A recent U.S. government study indicates that the average adult spends 84% of his or her life indoors, which is an environment of controlled temperature, light, humidity, and air circulation. In such environments, reality becomes determined by forces other than our own perceptions; television and commentators become our eyes. Reality becomes secondhand (Swan, 1992).

Yet it's the natural world and its finite resources that sustain all of life. Early introduction to environmental science is imperative in a world that will require future generations to use our limited resources wisely. Teachers of young children need to reflect on how they can become an instrumental part of future practices that will conserve and preserve our natural world. Teachers who model and encourage environmental stewardship for young children, showing them the interconnectedness of life, will be the life blood of tomorrow. Teachers working to awaken a sense of wonder and caring about the natural environment often find that this becomes an emotional journey (Carson, 1956).

Teachers need first to examine their own beliefs and feelings about the natural world before they can bring that world into perspective for students. An exercise that we do in my environmental awareness workshop begins with having the individuals reflect on what type of environment was a substantial part of their early years (rural, suburban, or urban). Each teacher reflects back to one of the earliest memories of his or her interactions with the natural world. We then group ourselves according to the different environmental settings and share early personal experiences with the natural world.

Someone from the city recalled the heat of the pavement in summer and hearing the "ping" of the alert chord at the gas station next door. Another remembered swinging on the front porch and listening to the wind. I remembered bringing the cows home in a thunder and lightning storm.

Over the years, there has been a consistent increase in the number of teachers in the urban group, while the rural group has almost disappeared. This finding helped us realize how artificial environments have become the dominant influences in our lives. Through discussion, we also discovered that early experiences that touched us at an emotional level usually centered on the animal world. With fewer opportunities to interact with the natural world, our own sense of wonder had become dulled over the years since childhood.

To become good role models for children, teachers also need to examine their fears of certain elements in nature (e.g., snakes, insects, etc.). The situation arose for me one day when a garter snake was brought in for "show-and-tell." I've never been fond of snakes because they don't move like I expect them to, and anything that sticks its tongue out at me is certainly suspect! I was alone with a group of 15 preschoolers when the snake slithered up over the coffee can container and into the hollow blocks. I dispelled my fear of the snake by realizing that the children were looking at me as a model. This was a major breakthrough for me.

Fear can be overcome by learning more about the critter that is feared. I discovered this one summer while on vacation in Canada. A neighbor asked me about a large green caterpillar that was spinning a cocoon over her doorway. While I had never taken a liking to the insect world, this situation intrigued me enough to do some research. I now consider myself the Cecropia moth expert and annually disseminate the giant silk moth to classrooms in our area. The children now call me, endearingly, "the bug lady"; and I have the joy of feeling an integral part of life's metamorphosis as I watch the moths emerge from their cocoons and pump up their wings into a full four-inch width of exquisite rust and white symmetry.

In addition to dealing with fears, we also need to revive and sharpen our own sensory awareness. Do we hear the bluejay warn with his imperative call, "Thief, thief," at our arrival in the woods? Do we fill our nostrils with the thick earthy smell of decaying leaves, feel the caress of snowflakes on our cheeks, listen to the stream as it tumbles over rocks on its way to the sea, and let ourselves be numbed by its bracing water? Companionship with life outdoors and an abiding love for nature need to be in the the teacher's heart. The rewards are contemplative, unhurried solace that puts daily living in perspective.

Developmental Characteristics and Implications for Curriculum

To understand the natural world, people must have firsthand experiences in that world. It is the earliest memories we have of that contact that most affect our later responses, images, and values. Exposure to phenomena in the natural world influences how young children perceive basic life processes and how they interact to formulate their own ideas of how things work.

We, as teachers, realize that our students should know about the interconnectedness of life, yet we continue to teach minilessons on plant germination, transpiration, hibernation, camouflage, dormancy, etc. The ubiquitous "ditto sheet" removes the student further from a direct hands-on experience of nature. Too often, there is no connection between nature education and math, social studies, literature, music, and art, not to mention the failure to go outside where it is all happening naturally. We know that all students learn in different ways, yet we use our texts and teacher's manuals as if they were the only recipe for learning. "We need to give kids a chance in school to enter the room by different windows, so to speak— but be able to see the relationships among the different windows" (Gardner, 1991, p.203).

Learning about interconnectedness begins in the classroom as we deal with a diversity of students. Diversity also exists in nature in rich abundance, waiting to be explored, questioned, and interpreted.

When we plan a curriculum, it's important to start at the children's level. As the children's world expands, they may feel overwhelmed and wonder how they fit into the scheme of things. Such concern is expressed in the following poem.

Who Am I

The trees ask me,
And the sky,
And the sea asks me
    Who am I?

The grass asks me,
And the sand,
And the rocks ask me
    Who am I?

The wind tells me
At nightfall,
And the rain tells me
    Someone small.

Someone small
Someone small
But a piece
    of
      it
        all.
            Felice Holman

One way to make ideas relevant to children is through the use of literature. For example, the book <u>Pezzettino</u> by Leo Lionni might be used to help children realize concepts related to who they are as individuals. The story is about a colored cube who sets out around the world to ask if he might be a piece of a larger entity such as "the Strong One" or "the Flying One." In his travels and questioning he comes to the re-

alization that he is whole in himself and is made of many parts. After reading this book, the children can create their own character collage from colored construction paper pieces and then tell their own stories.

It's also important to be aware of the children's perceptions of the natural world. While on a recent hike, we came upon a large oak tree, and as we watched, small twigs with clusters of oak leaves were floating down around the tree. The children wondered why. They had learned that the leaves are important in providing food for the tree and that leaves help clean the air. Now they were seeing leaves being destroyed. We looked up into the tree and there, scampering over the branches, was a black squirrel. The children spotted a cluster of twigs higher in the fork of the tree— obviously a squirrel home. The children scolded the squirrel for destroying parts of the tree and for being so wasteful with the leaves. One little boy looked for a while and then commented, "It looks like the tree got a hair cut," as he picked up one of the twigs for his collection.

While sense of self is important, so is the realization that it's through cooperation with others and our natural surroundings that we effect harmony. The Navaho song "The Earth Is Our Mother; We Must Take Care of Her" could be used to help children realize that the Earth is like a mother because of her life-giving sustenance. While the concept of Earth as mother may seem abstract to preschool children who feel their family is their whole world, introducing the idea while they are young plants the seed of a basic understanding that can mature over time.

When asked, young children can generally offer some ideas on how to preserve and protect the earth. The power of print can be demonstrated by writing down what the children say on a placard and letting them illustrate it. In doing this, every idea is accepted—even the idea offered about wanting to save the turtles (the Teenage Mutant Ninja kind!). The illustrated placards can be attached to long wrapping paper tubes and carried in procession through the different classrooms.

Nurturing a sense of caring for living things can be done by helping children see from another perspective. Puppets can be used effectively for this. A shy turtle, a slow snail, and an industrious beaver are just some of the coveted puppets the children begin to identify with. Each puppet has a distinct personality and can be used to impart factual information about the animal. Helping children see from another perspective can also be done through personifications.

One way to do this is to hold a "conversation" with a real animal in the environment. This might be done with Marshmallow, the litter-trained rabbit, or the spider dangling above the blocks. "Good morning, Marshmallow, are you hungry? Would you like a carrot for breakfast?" or "Charlotte, where is your web? Have you caught that pesky fly that has been buzzing around?"

Books are also good for giving perspective and fostering an awareness about needs and habitat. In Anne Mazer's book The Salamander Room, the questions the mother asks when her son brings home a salamander are questions we all might ask about a new creature in our life. "Where will he sleep?" "Where will he play?" "Will he miss his friends?" "How will you feed him?" With each question, the young boy in the story problem solves by reconstructing a habitat that is perfect for a happy salamander. In doing so, he discovers the interconnectedness of nature's elements, including water, plants, bugs, birds, and trees.

When we read The Fall of Freddie the Leaf by Leo Buscaglia—a story about the meaning of life and death—I have the children outside under a big sugar maple tree, stretched out in a leaf pile we previously constructed. As I read, the children look up into the maple's scant, leaf-clad branches for Freddie, the last leaf to fall because he is afraid of the unknown, especially death. All of our senses are heightened by this experience. Last fall this book was especially poignant, as our classroom bunny was trying to recover from an infected scratch from a cat. Despite all of our care and love, he did die. The experience, however, brought us closer together as a class, as we experienced the loss together. Another excellent book addressing the meaning of death is Lifetimes, by Bryan Mellonie and Robert Ingpen.

Hey! Get Off Our Train by John Burningham is a great book for learning about endangered species and destruction of habitat. It also lends itself well to dramatization. The children act out the different animals whose habitats have been destroyed and who are now seeking asylum aboard a dream train commandeered by a boy and his dog. The elephant pleads, "Please let me come with you on your train. Someone is coming to cut off my tusks, and soon there will be none of us left." The child playing the engineer loves having the power to rescue him from his plight. Dramatizing this type of story helps children become sensitive to the living world. This concept is reinforced every time we walk through the woods. The children are always reminded that the woods serve as home to many different animals and that we must be respectful of their home. If we enter the woods with respect, the animals may occasionally choose to show themselves to us.

Books can be used to increase sensitivity awareness. Arnold Lobel's book

Grasshopper on the Road is a humorous easy reader about a grasshopper who unknowingly takes a bite out of an apple only to find that he has destroyed the roof of a worm's house. The children giggle as they envision the humorous picture of an apple house turning upside down, putting the bathtub in the kitchen, and a worm yelling, "Help, my head is bumping on the walls!" as the apple rolls down the hill. This is a great book for showing different perspectives and the value of all life. Through this story, children are introduced to the concept that animals—such as the worms—have feelings, too.

Another excellent book that is highly fanciful but teaches accurate facts about insects is RoaldDahl's James and the Giant Peach. While it's a book with separate chapters, it's so well written that it kept a three-, five-, and seven-year-old all engrossed for almost an hour of reading.

Personification of living things can be done by the teacher as role model or by using appropriate books. The "Who Am I?" series (Santillana Publishing) is an excellent science and fiction series that subtly presents what important characteristics natural elements possess, while weaving a story that appeals to a young audience. There is a story about love and family relationships in the I Am a Tree book, along with the important information of how a tree grows, makes its own food, and survives. The forest is cut down and children are aware of the subtle message about destruction of natural resources. The I Am a Raindrop book follows the adventures of a drop of rain on its way to the sea, and along the way points out the pollution problem that we all are contributors to.

Teacher as Model

As teachers, we need to be dreamers and have a sense of vision. If we are con-cerned about the destruction of our natural resources, we can teach about recycling, reusing, and reducing the materials made from nonrenewable elements. It is important that we don't do this as isolated lessons but model the behavior in everything we do on a daily basis, such as using washable cups instead of paper, reusing paper, and sorting the refuse in the classroom. In nature when we are collecting we also try not to upset the natural balance. We only take things that we need and then only if there is a great abundance of the item. We always thank the tree for leaves, the plant for a dandelion flower, or crow for the feather lying on the ground. Such practices build true stewardship for the Earth and its inhabitants. They also capture the child's heart and imagination and, at the same time, impress him or her with the power for change that each of us possesses.

Knowledge is a collective product. In the process of gaining knowledge there needs to be much opportunity for "messing about" (exploration) with a teacher who is a facilitating pathfinder (Gardner, 1991). Teachers of young children need to let their childlike sense of wanting to know about the world around them be their guide. The children who are watching an earthworm stretch and shorten as it tries to find a dark moist haven under the ground are learning about a different method of locomotion as well as how light and moisture affect an earthworm's life. The teacher, as pathfinder, guides the children by asking related questions.

There are endless resources available to teachers in preparing for nature-related exploratory activities. Teachers need not be hampered by limited school budgets nor rely on the availability of "science kits" to introduce young people to the natural world. Nor is a rural setting required. Earthworms, soil, rocks, grasses or weeds, nests, leaves, seeds, insects, cocoons, sunlight, animals, and many other gifts of nature are right outside the door, no matter where a person lives. The teacher, as pathfinder, leads the children to these resources or incorporates them into the classroom for exploration. These natural elements, attractively displayed, draw curious children to them and are a great source of language development in the curriculum.

One important concept that underlies exploration of the natural world is that everything changes. The acceptance of this concept is an important lesson for young children who are often uncomfortable with change. If the concept of change is explored through dealing with the seasons, metamorphosis, animal behavior, and plant growth, young children come to understand the natural rhythm of change and how it is a part of time, life, and death.

Some changes take place over a long period of time and are difficult to conceptualize, while others are immediate and easily understood. After a nine-month wait for the giant silk moth cocoon to open, one young girl, with obvious joy, let the moth walk upon her hand and exclaimed to anyone who would listen, "This is probably a once in a lifetime happening and it happened to me!" In a young child's world everything is perceived from the self, and the teacher builds on this perception.

When a moth emerged from a cocoon, I seized the teachable moment and picked her up, telling her that she had been nine months in that cocoon and perhaps she didn't remember that she was once a caterpillar. I proceeded to carry her over to the book center and told her I would read her the story A Moth Is Born (by Herbert Walker). She balanced on my knee as I turned the pages and seemed content with the lilt of my voice. The intrigued children gathered around in complete fascination,

also listening to the story. As I read the last page of the book, the moth began the rapid wing flutter used in the courting process. I thanked her for the recognition and invited the children to simulate the wing flutter with their thumbs locked and fingers extended. The moth then took flight and landed on the art display hanging from the ceiling—much to the children's enjoyment.

Environmental education is also an international curriculum theme. When I was discussing environmental curriculum for early childhood with a director of a preschool in Moscow, she shared through a diagram (and an interpreter) how she based her school curriculum on the child as center and expanded in concentric circles including the child's home environment, family, the school environment, night and day, seasons, community, world, and space.

Using the Outdoors as a Classroom

Teachers are often intimidated by the thought of going outdoors and using an integrated curriculum approach. The first hurdle is "What do you do when there are no walls or boundaries?" I will never forget taking a class of three-year-olds outside before we had a playground. I said we would go for a walk and look for signs of spring. As soon as we were out the door a boy excitedly pointed to the church NO PARKING sign, announcing, "I found one." Soon after, another little boy started to run towards the woods several hundred yards behind the school at full speed, and, of course, the entire class started to follow him. With a certain amount of panic, I proceeded to gather them together again. I quickly realized the need to plan and communicate in developmentally appropriate language the activity or focus before leaving the building.

It is imperative to build group cooperation and trust in the teacher before attempting an outdoor classroom experience. A class that thinks together, cares for one another, and respects the teacher as a role model will be a joy to take anywhere. This can be accomplished in many subtle ways.

When a teacher shows respect for individual differences and plans for those differences by incorporating the unique characteristics of each child to advantage, group cohesiveness begins. One child may be a natural leader and another have very sharp eyes, while another is very helpful. One year in summer outdoor education, the class envisioned themselves as a Native American tribe. We learned that in some tribes animals were symbols for different character traits. I made up some badges with the stamped pictures of the animals on them. When we were on a hike the children were working toward earning a badge that each wanted. Some of the animal symbols from the Haudenosaunee Nations were the BEAVER—symbolizing working together and following guidance of elders; the DEER—symbolizing endurance, harmony, breathing, and listening; and the WOLF—symbolizing the trailblazers seeking to understand the unknown. One girl, who always had difficulty keeping up with the tribe, was thrilled to receive the deer badge for endurance; and an active, easily distracted boy treasured his badge for following the guidance of the teachers.

Another activity that involves group cooperation is the dramatization of the music from the recording Spin Spider Spin (Zetlin& Berman, 1974). I put the music on indoors and as the recording describes how a spider spins a web, the children take thick rug yarn and start attaching it to different structures. The abilities of all children are utilized in this activity as they learn about gravity, balance, tying skills, and—best of all—cooperation to build a structure that will entrap the butterfly, as played by

the teacher, when finished. We then do this activity outside in a grove of trees with a tape recording of the music. Several of the younger children were happy to be baby spiders and lie in wait for the parents to finish the web and secure dinner. Some children decided to be yellow jackets and aggressively attack the web and spiders. When I asked them how a bee stings and where the stinger was located, we had to do some research, only to find that the stinger protrudes from the back. From then on they needed to back into the web, and that controlled wild aggression.

There are many activities that help build group cooperation. A good resource is Sharing Nature with Children by JosephCornell. One activity I use frequently to teach interdependence is his game on webbing. This game emphasizes the essential interrelationships among all members of nature's community. To play the game, the children form a circle. The leader stands inside the circle, with a ball of string. The leader starts by asking, "Who can name a plant that grows in this area?" Someone might answer, "Grass." The leader recognizes the response with "Good. Here, Miss Grass, you hold the end of the string." The game continues by the leader asking, "Is there an animal living around here that might eat the grass?" . . . "Bugs." . .. "Y es, bugs might eat the grass. Here, Mr. Bugs, you hold the string here; you are connected to Miss Grass by your need for food. Now, who might need Mr. Bugs for lunch?" The game thus continues connecting the children with string as their relationships to the rest of the group emerge. While the game starts with a focus on food, other elements are also brought in as well—elements such as other animals, soil, water, air, etc.—until the entire circle of children is connected, symbolizing the web of life. Interconnectedness is further emphasized by adding another dimension to the game. One member of the web is removed through some plausible means—e.g., a fire or a logger kills a tree. The person playing the tree falls to the ground while still holding on to the string. Anyone who feels a tug on his or her string when the tree falls is in some way affected by the death of the tree. The next step is to have everyone who felt a tug from the falling tree give a tug. This process continues until everyone experiences the effect of the destruction of the tree.

Forming partnerships within the group is another important structural activity ensuring group cohesiveness. This can be done in a number of ways. I use random pairing if possible and make modifications if a match is a volatile one. I combine the children's senses with the pairing activity by preparing a "feely bag" with natural objects that I wish the children to learn more about. For example, while working from the "Trees are Terrific!" section in Earth Child (Sheehan& W aidner, 1991), I fill the bag with two of each: bark (smooth and rough), fruits, seeds, wood rounds, fungus, leaves, and moss. Each child in turn reaches into the bag and describes the object after a tactile exploration. They remove the object after we have made some guesses as to what it might be and keep it until everyone has an item. Children with the same items are paired. The children love the anticipation of guessing who their partner will be by listening to like descriptions and then are sometimes surprised when their partner is not whom they guessed. I then tell them that they are responsible for their partner on our hike, and I model that responsibility with my own partner. If we become separated, I sing "Lost my partner, what will I do?" to the tune of "Skip to My Loo." This always brings partners back or alerts me to other partners who might have strayed.

We have waded in streams, caught crayfish and bug larvae, have gone fishing and had treasure hunts, watched stars and fireflies, hugged trees, and rescued young animals. Our motto is "A hunting we will go. We'll catch a bug (or fish, etc.), make a wish, and then we'll let him go." We even went on an overnight outing with parents and prepared meals at the site.

The outdoors should be explored in all seasons. Integrative activities such as paper making, tending a compost heap, gardening, making maple syrup, or sledding (if it is a regional possibility) provide the hands-on learning for nature interconnectedness. Children having these experiences will become intimately aware of their natural surroundings and feel a real part of it all.

Thoughts and Recommendations for Outdoor Education

Following are some thoughts on using the outdoors as a classroom, formulated over many years of teaching outdoor education to young children. They can be modified to fit individual teaching styles.

- Emphasize learning by doing, discovering, smelling, touching, or playing a game. This approach is generally more effective and long lasting than learning by listening to a lecture.
- Let your group teach you, and acknowledge this to the group.
- Encourage curiosity. Let the children find their own items of interest.
- Encourage questioning. Be a "question asker" as a model, but beware of seeking "right" and "wrong" answers.
- Be willing to get dirty.
- Remember to bring your sense of humor.
- Be ready to work with unexpected situations—don't disregard that mushroom just because you are on a bird walk.

- Conversely, don't lose sight of your objectives and the processes you want to stress.
- Learn a few common names of plants, animals, etc. It will help the group understand the interrelationships in an environment. Learning a few names is not difficult; but don't worry if you don't know a name.
- Show children how to use field guides. Make this a part of the learning process.
- Be careful with identification. Labels are usually forgotten, can create a distance, and can be difficult for those of limited intellectual abilities. It is more important to identify what it smells like, what it feels like, where it grows, etc.
- Maintain a leader/student ratio of 1:9 or less for best results in the outdoors. Parents and other teachers can be utilized if they have been oriented to your outdoor education approach.
- Speak in terms the children can understand. Relate their outdoor experience to home, family, peer group experiences, and other things familiar to the children.
- Try to use all of your senses, and teach the children to do the same.
- Be cautious when touching and tasting. Never taste anything you are not sure of. Be certain you and your group are able to identify poison ivy and/or poison oak.
- Relate outdoor excursions to the regular classroom experience. Adequate pre-site orientation and post-site review are critical.
- Treat every living thing with kindness. Try not to disturb the balance of nature when collecting things for study.
- When possible, let the children play in the natural setting with natural materials, in and out of the classroom. Follow their lead for they are the natural scientists.

- Because guest specialists often have difficulty relating to young children, be prepared to help the guest focus on things relevant to your group, often by rephrasing and simplifying what they say.
- Keep safety in mind at all times. When walking single file along a stream bank, consider using a long knotted rope with eighteen knots, so that each child can space him- or herself appropriately. Let the children know what you expect of them, but avoid introducing too many rules at once. It's best to explain the rules as they are needed. Identify poison ivy immediately and follow the rule, "Leaflets three, let them be." For bees in flowers, you might use, "Leave them alone and they will fly on home" (from the song "That Is the Way of the Bees," on the <u>Spin Spider Spin</u> album). Be aware of children's allergies, and have a first aid kit and Red Cross-trained adult on all outings. Model relaxed exploration and enjoyment. Remember that accidents are more prone to happen when the leader is apprehensive.
- Remember that community resources are an important part of any environmental education program. Tap into these resources. Places to visit are the school yard, the neighborhood, nearby parks, forests, ponds, or streams. Natural history museums, zoos, aquariums, farms, water treatment plants, recycling plants, and children's museums are founts of information; some more hands-on than others. Resource people can be found at universities and colleges, nature centers and preserves, parks, and your library.
- Keep in mind the following understandings as you work with young children in the out-of-doors. Let these understandings guide your plans, actions, and interactions.

1. *Children cannot play with or be in nature without physical involvement. The natural world beckons the child to act upon it, engaging all the senses.*

2. *The natural world stimulates creativity, inviting the child to use his or her own ideas.*

3. *Imaginative and dramatic play are stimulated by the availability, familiarity and flexible character of natural materials.*

4. *Natural materials allow the child to work on the concepts of power, strength, love, and caring.*

Summary

As teachers of young children, we need to be models for interaction with the natural environment. We need to examine how we feel about nature and be honest about our feelings. Children will respect that honesty. We need to understand the children's perspective and be accepting.

We may have preplanned agendas, but we can't let them get in the way of that teachable moment, when a child's understanding is at its height because of an emotional involvement with a natural wonder.

Curriculum must be integrative, just as everything in nature is. With young children, it's appropriate to include sense-heightening experiences that will be the building blocks for all later learning.

We are not experts, but learners together, exclaiming beauty, seeing through the eyes of others, caring, and sharing a small part of a very big home, our Planet Earth!

References

Burningham, J. (1989). Hey! Get off the train. New York: Crown Publishers.

Buscaglia, L. (1982). The fall of Freddie the leaf. Austin, TX: Holt, Rinehart, & Winston.

Carson, R. (1956). The sense of wonder. New York: Harper & Row.

Cornell, J. (1979). Sharing nature with children. Nevada City, CA: Ananda Publications.

Dahl, R. (1983). James and the giant peach. New York: Penguin.

Gardner, H. (1991). The unschooled mind. New York: Basic Books.

Holman, F. Source Unknown. (Workshop handout.)

Lionni, L. (1975). Pezzettino. New York: Pantheon Books.

Lobel, A. (1978). Grasshopper on the road. New York: Harper & Row.

Mazer, A. (1991). The salamander room. New York: Alfred A. Knopf.

Mellonie, B., & Ingpen, R. (1983). Lifetimes. New York: Bantam Books.

Santillana Publishing Co. (1974). Who am I series. New York: Santillana Publishing.

Sheehan, K., & Waidner, M. (1991). Earth child. Tulsa, OK: Council Oak Books.

Swan, J. A. (1992). Nature as teacher and healer. New York: Villard Books.

Walker, H. (1957). A moth is born. Chicago: Rand McNally.

Zetlin, P., & Berman, M. (1974). Spin spider spin. Freeport, NY: Educational Activities. LP recording.

When the bird and the book disagree, always believe the bird.

Birdwatcher's Proverb

IV.
People and Programs

Nature's Way Preschool
Ruth A. Wilson, Ph.D.

Section Overview

Presented in this section is a description of an early childhood environmental education program offered as ongoing preschool at a nature center. One obvious advantage of housing a preschool at a nature center is access to the natural surroundings typically found at such sites.

Program Overview

Nature's Way Preschool is a unique nine-month program for three-, four-, and five-year-old children. The school is operated by the Kalamazoo Nature Center in Kalamazoo, Michigan. One of the first things a visitor to the school would notice is the secluded setting. This comes as a surprise to a first-time visitor, as the address for the preschool indicates that it's located on a heavily traveled highway near the edge of the city. A driveway surrounded by trees and grass leads the visitor from the noise and traffic of the roadway into a parking lot, deliberately situated some distance from the entrance of the school building. A row of trees separates the campus of the school from the busy highway and the city beyond. A sidewalk leads from the parking lot across a grassy area and back to a cabin, which is framed by a forest of trees. This cabin houses the Nature's Way Preschool. Nowhere in sight can one find flashy signs or brightly painted playground equipment.

The program at Nature's Way Preschool matches the setting. It's informal, warm, and welcoming. Its focus is on closeness to nature. Materials inside the classroom reflect and encourage an active interest in nature. There are children's books about nature, an aquarium, a worm box, posters about nature, animal puppets, a variety of stuffed animals, potted plants, and small animal figurines (all realistic versus cartoon-type characters). Children's drawings of flowers, trees, animals, and other nature-related themes decorate the room.

Children arriving for the day come into the classroom accompanied by a parent or caregiver. Each is greeted by name and a warm welcome. Each child carries a book bag labelled with his or her name. Often children bring something from home that they'd like to share with the group. One day a yellow jacket is brought in, carefully sheltered in a small box lined with tissues. The bee is not alive, but its body is intact. Andrew wants to examine it more closely with a magnifying glass. His mother cautions Andrew to hold the bee gently, as its wings are fragile. As Andrew and his mother examine the bee, they talk about having found a similar bee in their garage.

After the children have had 10 to 15 minutes of exploring new or familiar things in the classroom, their teacher, Ann, invites them to gather in the center of the room for circle time. The children and two teacher assistants readily move to the circle in anticipation of the activities and materials Ann has prepared for the day. One assistant actively participates in the group activity and encourages the children to do the same, while the other takes notes about the children's participation. She makes notes about who has had a turn for a desired activity and who hasn't; she makes notes about what the children say regarding their interests, likes, and dislikes; and she keeps a record of any special concerns. These notes are then used for ideas on how to meet individual needs.

An important part of the program is helping each child feel that he or she is special. One activity that reflects and reinforces this concept during circle time is a discussion of who's present and who's absent. When Andrew reported that Steven was absent because he broke his ankle, a teacher assistant immediately asked the children if they knew what Steven's favorite color was. After the children reported "yellow," she went to the cupboard and got a large yellow piece of paper, indicating to the children that she would fold it into the shape of a card and that they could then sign it or draw a picture on it to send "get well" wishes to Steven.

Another way in which children are made to feel important is through respect for their individual choices. Children are given choices as to what they would like to do and how they would like to do it. These choices are honored as long as they also reflect a respect for others in the classroom. One hour out of a two-and-one-half-hour session is devoted to Center Exploration. It's during this time that children are free to participate in activities of their own choosing, and thus a time when many activities occur simultaneously. Some children may be painting while others are looking at books. Some children are doing puzzles or building with blocks, while others are playing with toy animals. Some children may be examining the worm bin and aquarium, while others are "cooking over a campfire" in the dramatic play area.

Curriculum

The curriculum at Nature's Way Preschool is based on a philosophy that expresses concern for young children and the natural environment. This philosophy is stated in their brochure:

> *We want children to have fun learning about themselves and the natural and man-made surroundings, while becoming aware of their own potential and their relationships to their environments, including other people. Our program combines traditional readiness-learning and pre-school activities with environmental education programs. Nature's Way Preschool teaches the child by providing experiences that develop mind, body, and spirit.*

Caring and thoughtfulness are stressed throughout the day—caring for each other, caring for the school environment, and caring for the natural world. While the curriculum at Nature's Way Preschool fosters growth across all developmental areas (language, physical development, self-help skills, concept development, social interaction, aesthetic development, etc.), the central theme is expressed by their motto—"Learning about ourselves and the rest of the world—Nature's Way." Nature-related experiences are incorporated into all aspects of the program—in songs, stories, art, outdoor explorations, games, puzzles, dramatic play, room decorations, etc. A variety of nature-related themes are introduced on a monthly basis. Following is a listing of typical themes for the different months of the year.

September: Recycling, apples, autumn
October: Habitats, pumpkins, spiders, Halloween
November: Migration, hibernation, Native Americans, turkeys
December: Winter, snow, celebrations, pine trees and cones, reindeer, gifts
January: Winter animals and tracks, solar system, dinosaurs
February: Groundhog day, valentines, senses
March: Weather, St. Patrick's Day, spring (buds, birds returning, maple sugaring)
April: Wildflowers, planting and seeds, insects, bunnies, chicks
May: Barnyard, pond life, Mother's Day

Many of the ideas for the themes and related activities are from a resource book, Teaching Young Children Using Themes. This book, edited by Marjorie Kostelink and published by Michigan State University, includes sections on plants, sky, rocks, insect, dinosaurs, wild birds, bears, and water. Other favorite resources used by Ann and her teacher assistants include Love the Earth by Patty Claycomb and an audio recording, We All Live Together. Love the Earth is published by Partner Press and offers a variety of both indoor and outdoor environmental activities for young children. We All Live Together is a four-volume set of songs and activities, developed and performed by Steve Millang and Greg Scelsa. Included on the albums are such nature-related songs as "The World Is a Rainbow," "Months of the Year," and "It's a Beautiful Day"—all performed in a pop-rock musical style.

In addition to an extended free-choice time (usually about an hour), the daily routine also includes "group time" where children participate in a variety of games and other activities. Examples include the "Seed Game" and the "Speckled Frogs." For the "Seed Game," Ann reaches into her bag of prepared materials and gives individual children laminated pictures of flowers, seeds, sunshine, and raindrops. Children listen as a song is sung, and on cue, stand up and role-play the part indicated by the picture they hold in their hands. The following words are sung to the tune of the "I'm a Little Teapot" song: "I'm a little seed deep in the ground. Warmed by the sunshine yellow and round. Cooled by the raindrops falling down. Time to raise my head and look around." From this song and activity, children can learn several different nature-related concepts: plants grow from seeds; the rain and the sun help plants to grow; growing often means changing and getting bigger; change is a part of nature.

Closeness to nature is also reflected in the materials and the physical environment. Objects from nature are used to decorate the classroom; windows and doors are kept open as long as the weather permits; and live plants and animals are considered important parts of the classroom. Respect for the natural environment is also reflected through attention to conservation and recycling. In using water, paper, glue, and other materials, the children are encouraged to use only what they need and to take care of all the materials and equipment in the classroom. Recycled materials are used extensively in the arts and crafts projects, and, whenever possible, for other activities as well. Throwaways (such as paper plates, cups, etc.) are rarely used.

Children's books play a big role in the curriculum at Nature's Way Preschool. The children's library in the classroom is stocked with a variety of books with positive nature-related themes. Included are children's stories, such as The Very Busy Spider and The Very Hungry Caterpillar by

Eric Carle. Other commonly used authors are Lydia Dabcovich (author of Sleepy Bear and other books) and Jan Brett (author of The Mitten, etc.). Also included are Nature Series books, such as the "My First Wildlife Books" and books from the "Eyewitness Juniors" series.

Teacher Qualifications

The teacher in the Nature's Way Preschool is, first of all, an early childhood educator. Because of the program's focus on learning about nature, she is also an environmental educator. Formal training requirements, however, are in the area of early childhood education. The following position announcement outlines the qualifications and job description for the early childhood teacher position and emphasizes the importance of an early childhood background.

Preschool Coordinator/Environmental Educator. Responsibilities: implement all aspects of the education program including administrative responsibilities; preschool curriculum development and daily teaching; coordinate all business, clerical, and supervisor aspects of the position. Qualifications: Bachelor's in elementary education, environmental education or related field (12 hrs. of early childhood education as mandated by the Dept. of Social Services); knowledge of developmental skills in the education of young children along with a desire and ability to relate to very young children; experience in early elementary education; able to communicate effectively and comfortably with parents; competency in oral/written communication; able to develop/organize/manage a number of tasks; personal commitment to Kalamazoo Nature Center's mission.

Ann Yunger, who presently serves as the teacher/director of Nature's Way Preschool, is working on her master's degree in early childhood education and has experience as a nature educator through her work with the summer programs at the Kalamazoo Nature Center.

Parent Involvement

Parents are considered an important part of the program at Nature's Way Preschool. A "theme calendar," sent home on a monthly basis, contains information about planned activities and concepts. A monthly newsletter is also sent home outlining, in more detail, information about special projects, field trips, and ideas for activities to do at home. Parents are also invited to visit at any time and to stay with their child for at least the first five or ten minutes of each session.

Parents seem excited about the program at Nature's Way Preschool. Once one sibling has been enrolled in the program, other siblings tend to follow. One parent, who now works as a teacher assistant in the program, has had two children in Nature's Way Preschool. Her older son, now eight years old, still talks about his experiences in the preschool and shows a strong interest in nature. When given a choice of participating in a summer nature program or a science and math camp, he chose the nature program. His mother was not surprised and feels that his interest in nature stems from his positive experiences at Nature's Way Preschool.

Time Outdoors

Every day at Nature's Way Preschool includes time outdoors. Often, children use this time to run and play freely in the open areas. There's a lot to explore, as the school is surrounded by an eight-acre campus. Most of the area is "natural" versus "developed." In addition to a large grassy area, the campus also includes woods, a stream, thickets, and a sand and stone pile where children are free to dig and "mess around." Children use their outdoor time to climb on logs, make piles of leaves, and dig in the dirt. They collect "pretty" stones, watch the chipmunk in the bushes, and dance with the wind. Sometimes, they walk along the path that follows the stream through the woods. In the spring, they plant seedlings and look for animals in and near the pond. Throughout every season of the year, they watch for changes in the trees, the weather, and animal behavior. And always, they learn to look with wonder and to tread with care.

The Beginner's Nature Program
Marcie Oltman

Section Overview

This section describes an early childhood environmental education program offered as an ongoing pre-school at the New Canaan Nature Center in Connecticut. Marcie Oltman, who wrote this section, served as a teacher in this program for several years. A subsection defines the meaning of active learning, a critical component of the early childhood program. This subsection was originally published in the Nature Center newsletter, to help parents better understand the program.

Program Overview

A three-year-old on a preschool outing spies a dragonfly delicately perched on a cattail reed. Her excitement is barely contained as she races back to get her mother and proudly exclaims, "Look, Mom! I found nature!"

This revelation was the proverbial "light bulb" going on in the mind of a three-year-old. The joy of that personal discovery could not have been more obvious. The moment was especially poignant in that it occurred during a parent visit at a unique preschool operated by the New Canaan Nature Center in New Canaan, Connecticut.

In operation since the fall of 1967, the Beginner's Nature Program (BPN) is a fully licensed preschool for three-, four-, and five-year-old children, which emphasizes direct sensory experiences in the natural world. Beginning with a modest public program for neighborhood children, the Nature Cen-

ter gradually established the preschool in response to a growing need for quality early childhood education. Currently, the program is in high demand—enrollment is at the facility's capacity of 90 children with an ever-growing waiting list. The Nature Center has also expanded its early childhood offerings to include an extensive summer nature camp for preschoolers and a very popular parent/toddler program.

The program's uniqueness stems from a strong commitment to both environmental education and active learning. (See accompanying article.) Based upon seasonal changes, the broad-based curriculum includes art, music, perceptual and cognitive skill development, large and small motor skill development, natural science exploration, and, most importantly, daily walks through the Center's diverse habitats.

These daily hikes and outdoor experiences are the cornerstone of the program. While other preschools have outdoor components normally limited to artificial play structures and fenced-in yards, BNP children experience the freedom of casual exploration, unencumbered by swing sets and jungle gyms. Mini-adventures occur on every inch of the Nature Center's 40 acres of meadows, forests, ponds, and marshes. It is this aspect that really defines the uniqueness of the program. Eve Ameer, director of Children's Programs at the Center, elaborates: "We provide children with positive daily experiences in the outdoors, encouraging individual and group exploration while enhancing the development of large motor skills and cooperative play. These experiences come at a crucial time in a child's development and internalization of values, and it is our hope that they reinforce our children's understanding and appreciation of the natural world."

Environmental education is, indeed, the focus on the BNP. Even with preschoolers, however, environmental education goes beyond creating an awareness and appreciation of the natural world. Like any quality environmental education program, it encompasses values, knowledge, beliefs, awareness, attitudes, skills, active participation, investigation, and above all the willingness and ability to combine these components into positive action toward the environment.

Specific objectives of the Beginner's Nature Program are (a) to instill in young children a sense of wonder for the natural environment, (b) to help young children grow in understanding of the natural environment, and (c) to help young children learn to take care of the natural environment. Two basic understandings provide direction and impetus to program implementation. The first understanding is that young children need direct experiences with the natural environment to grow in understanding and appreciation of it. A second understanding is that an appreciation for the natural environment needs to be fostered early in life.

The Beginner's Nature Program uses all of the aforementioned components to instill love for the environment. "We increase knowledge by creating insects with three body parts and six legs; we investigate biodegradability by burying plastic and paper and digging them up later for comparison studies; we participate in spring cleanup by collecting litter along the Nature Center's trails and displaying a collage of it; we increase our awareness by taking daily exploratory hikes; and we even take positive action by using recycled materials for nearly all of our arts and crafts projects," says Ameer.

The most exciting and significant aspect of this unique preschool is that all of these environmental education goals are accomplished while addressing the whole child with individual developmental needs.

Environmental education is synthesized with a developmentally appropriate curriculum framework for early childhood education derived from Piagetian theory. While the BNP has developed its own curriculum, it also incorporates various aspects of the High/Scope model, an internationally recognized program for early childhood education.

Through this synthesis, the BNP provides an environment in which children have opportunities to actively explore and the freedom to make choices. A consistent daily routine is followed. Each day there is a "work time" component, when children are encouraged to explore the classroom environment and engage in a variety of self-selected activities. Cleanup, bathroom, snack, music, and story time are followed by a learning circle in which hands-on nature lessons provide an introduction to a specific ecological concept or component. The day is capped with nature walks and outdoor play. Environmental education is successfully integrated into the curriculum, not as a separate subject but infused into art, music, science, pre-math, pre-reading, and language subject areas with unsurpassed commitment. Social, emotional, language, perceptual, cognitive, large motor, and small motor skills are all addressed in both the indoor and outdoor activity components of the program.

A favorite and illustrative activity in the curriculum is the "bird zip-line" nature lesson. During work time, each child may choose to make pretend binoculars out of two toilet-paper tubes fastened together. Upon bringing them to the circle, children are introduced to cardboard cutouts of migrating bird species, with a discussion on how to identify them by shape, size, and coloration. The children and teachers then lie on their backs, while focusing their binoculars on a string zip-line stretched above them. Suddenly, among shrieks of delight and "I saw its . . ." a bird cutout zips down the line on its imaginary way to a more southern locale. Soon these novice birders are ready to take their binoculars outside for a try at the "real thing."

Program Schedule

Ideally designed as a two-year program, children enter the preschool when they are three years old as "Discoverers." (Many children have already been introduced to the Nature Center through the very successful parent/toddler programs, "Nurturing Nature" and "Natural Wonders.") "Discoverers" meet two mornings (Tuesday and Thursday), three mornings (Monday, Wednesday, and Friday), or three afternoons (Monday, Tuesday, and Thursday) per week. Each class is limited to 14 children with two supervising teachers. Children return the next year as "Explorers," attending either five mornings or three afternoons per week. Explorer classes are limited to 16 children with two supervising teachers. Each class is three hours in length and operates on a schedule similar to the local schools, opening every year in mid-September and running through May.

Facilities

The Beginner's Nature Program is housed in the lower floor of the main activities building at the New Canaan Nature Center. Two classrooms are permanently arranged and equipped as the preschool, complete with delightfully painted nature murals on each wall. These classrooms are also used for day camp during the summer months. Other adjacent facilities include two bathrooms, a small kitchen, cubbie and reception areas, and a teacher resource room. An auditorium, the Center's hands-on Discovery Center, and a teaching greenhouse are additional educational resources utilized by the preschool.

Staff

The preschool is administered by a director of Children's Programs (Eve Ameer) who oversees all early childhood education programs at the Center. Ten permanent staff are employed in the program with the addition of two teaching interns and many parent participants. Each staff member has a college degree with an emphasis on early childhood education. Special events with other Nature Center teachers/naturalists are scheduled on a monthly and seasonal basis, and include live animal demonstrations and observations, maple sugaring, apple cidering, and horticultural projects.

Funding

The preschool functions as one of the many programs that the Nature Center of-fers. As such, it's an integral part of the Center's operations, not a separate entity. Tuition payments based on the number of days per week a child is enrolled go into the general operating budget of the Nature Center, and the BNP is allocated funds from that budget. An annual art show and silent auction is organized as a special fund-raiser to help supplement the preschool budget.

Registration

The application process for registration begins a full nine months before the child begins school in September. An open-house parent orientation and classroom visitation is scheduled in January, along with individual meetings with each parent and child to discuss the specifics of the program. There are generally many more applicants than spaces available—usually about a 4:1 ratio. Therefore, interviews are conducted to acquaint parents with the school's philosophy and to screen for families with compatible needs, interests, and philosophies. Interested parents submit application forms, a registration fee, and a copy of the child's birth certificate. Class rosters are finalized in early February. Children must be three or four by mid-September of the year they enter the program.

Parent Involvement

A variety of options invite active parent involvement in the Beginner's Nature Program. Written information about the program's philosophy and activities is shared on an ongoing basis; parent workshops are held periodically; volunteer opportunities are always available; parent/child sessions are provided; and a parent council provides advisory input into the ongoing operation of the program. Families are also invited to participate in the other educational programs offered through the New Canaan Nature Center.

Special Advantages

Because the Beginner's Nature Program is operated as an integral part of the New Canaan Nature Center, both the Center and the preschool enjoy many special advantages. First, a long-term relationship is established with the families of children in the preschool. This relationship continues well after the children have completed the program. Often, parents' environmental ethics and actions are influenced by witnessing their child's enthusiasm and knowledge of nature. Many of these parents continue their personal involvement as volunteers, staff, and board members of the Nature Center long after their children have completed the preschool program.

The ongoing relationship between the families and the preschool also benefits the children. They can expand on their preschool experience through summer camp, public programs and events, school programs, and volunteer opportunities well into their high school years and beyond. This type of long-term involvement with families is rare in an age of "assembly line" programming so common in nature centers today.

A second advantage is that the preschool has access to innumerable and diverse resources that it could not afford if operated as a separate entity. Access to special facilities, additional personnel, and a large land base create a program with more diversity and opportunity than what is available to the average preschool.

A third advantage is that both the Center and the preschool benefit from an extensive membership support system. Preschool families continue their financial support to the Center even after their children have graduated from the preschool. Likewise, the preschool has access to the Center's membership base in recruitment efforts.

The preschool program has been operating at the New Canaan Nature Center for over 25 years. It started with, and continues to receive, strong support from the Center's staff, board of trustees, and local community.

Summary

The New Canaan Nature Center's Beginner's Nature Program believes that providing children with nature-related skills and experiences during the formative preschool years will prove to be a crucial part of the creation of an environmentally responsible and sensitive adult. The ultimate goal of the program is to see that every child can exclaim with unrestrained enthusiasm, "Look, Mom! I found nature!"

Ingredients for Active Learning
Eve Ameer
Director of Children's Programs
New Canaan Nature Center

Young children discover and make sense of their world through experience, by constructing knowledge through their own actions. Learning is an active process. The Nature Center's preschool, the Beginner's Nature Program (BNP), provides a model for active learning in early childhood. One of the underlying objectives of our program for three-, four-, and five-year-olds is to provide an environment in which children will have the opportunity to explore actively and the freedom to make choices. Based on seasonal changes, the BNP curriculum includes natural science exploration and trail walks through the Nature Center. Classroom science, art, music and movement activities, and daily learning circles provide active learning experiences that reinforce our children's understanding and appreciation of the natural world.

Piaget's theories about how children think and learn provide an important guideline for defining the role of the teacher or parent in early childhood education. To help children learn and grow intellectually, we must first understand that thought comes from actions, not from words. Children learn best from concrete experience, or from "doing" rather than "hearing about." Instead of being dispensers of knowledge in the traditional sense, teachers and parents should serve as facilitators, providing opportunities for the child to act on his or her environment. BNP staff do not **teach** young children but, rather, **support children's learning.** Teachers in the BNP must be creative and observant, providing a variety of experiences and materials for children to explore and act upon.

As preschool educators and as parents, we play a critical role in helping young children become effective active learners. Active learning is more than just handling materials. Active learning occurs when all of the following ingredients are present: **materials** for your child, **manipulation** of those materials, **choice** by the child of what to try with which materials, **words** chosen and used by the child to describe what he or she is doing, and **support** by adults or other children in the form of recognition or questions that help the child think about his or her actions.

The role of the parent or preschool teacher is to encourage and help the child discover relationships between objects and actions, to learn from hands-on experiences. Parents and teachers can focus attention on the process by asking such open-ended questions as: What do you think happened?" "What did you do to make this happen?" "What is happening now?" and "What do you think would happen if . . .?" In this way, adults can encourage the child to think about and to predict the outcome of his or her actions, supporting the use of language to represent and expand the child's thinking.

Action is doing: playing, exploring, inventing, changing, moving, mixing, comparing, pretending, pouring, feeling, touching, choosing. Action is using your entire body to learn, interacting with other children and adults. The most significant long-term effect of active learning is learning how to learn. Solving problems, assuming responsibility, taking initiative, being creative, making plans—all involve cognitive processes that are developed through active explorations and experience in making choices. The most essential contribution we as parents and teachers can make to our children's education is to teach them **how** to learn rather than **what** to learn.

Young Naturalist Center
Ruth A. Wilson, Ph.D., and Marti Harmon, Ph.D.

Section Overview

This section describes a unique early childhood environmental education program offered as an ongoing preschool in the home and yard of Marti Harmon in California. The curriculum for this program combines multicultural education, environmental education, and early childhood education. One of its major goals is to foster in young children an appreciation and respect of beauty and diversity in the human and natural community.

Program Overview

The Young Naturalist Center is a family home day care program in Los Angeles, California, founded in 1983 by Dr. Marti Harmon. The entire curriculum at the Young Naturalist Center focuses on nature education or environmental education and emphasizes the interconnectedness of all living things as a way of life.

The program at the Young Naturalist Center focuses on the "wonder of life" and encourages children to stay in touch with their "inborn sense of wonder"—a sense that provides the impetus to explore the world around them. The Young Naturalist Center provides a safe, nurturing environment where children learn to interact and become at one with the natural world around them.

Children at the Young Naturalist Center are free to discover and create in a natural setting. They come to know this environment as a safe place to be—a place that is meant to be enjoyed and cultivated, but also treated with respect and never abused. The environment at the Young Naturalist Center reflects the balanced, harmonious structure of nature itself, where, like the very young of the animal kingdom, children are guided to an awareness of everything around them—what is safe or not safe; what is useful, edible, wearable, and what is not. The child's experience of such an environment leads to an understanding and respect for the structure of nature—a structure with rules that are necessary for the coexistence of all living things, rules that are as reasonable as they are demanding.

Children at the Young Naturalist Center are encouraged to experience the natural world through their senses in a variety of ways. They learn to see the wind blowing, hear the ants singing, taste and smell the change of seasons, feel flowers and butterflies. They are also encouraged to learn about the natural world through di-

rect participation in gardening, story dances, craft making, and creative dramatic play. They are given opportunities to burrow in underground tunnels, to nest in a field of tall grasses, and to rest in the branches of a tree. They are also introduced to the world of nature through ancient stories, folktales, and legends.

The program at the Young Naturalist Center reflects a concern for the physical, emotional, and spiritual well-being of the present and future generations. It seeks to educate young children in ways that preserve their natural heritage and, at the same time, prepare them for the realities of life in a complex, interrelated world. In an effort to keep the program relevant to the children and their families, parents, teachers, and the community are considered partners in developing the curriculum. Local community members research, design, and share culturally relevant ideas and materials with the children and teachers at the Young Naturalist Center.

Children who come to the Young Naturalist Center soon come to regard the Center as "theirs"—a place where they are

in harmony with nature, each other, and the few adults who are privileged to be their guides. The young children perceive themselves as caregivers and students of the Earth and all its creatures. They learn that what they do to the natural environment affects how they treat themselves and each other.

The overall goal of the Young Naturalist Center is to bring together people who envision a world without racial and cultural barriers, while creating an appreciation and understanding of the rich and diverse gifts they all bring to the human family. The curriculum designed to accomplish this goal blends environmental, holistic education with the spiritual knowing that has kept traditional cultures alive and in touch with the natural environment for centuries. Ideally, a child's experiences at the Young Naturalist Center will instill a deep sense of personal harmony that not only sees the possibility of a peaceful world, but can make that vision a reality.

The setting for the Young Naturalist Center is the backyard of Marti Harmon's home in Studio City, California. Marti's backyard differs dramatically from most of the backyards in her residential area just a few miles northeast of Los Angeles. This backyard features a variety of fruit trees, a large sand area equipped with buckets and shovels, a "theater area" with tree stump seats, a teepee and several small wooden hutches, a picnic table furnished with lumps of modeling clay, an assortment of buckets and watering cans, and piles of stuffed animals. It is in this setting that young children learn about rain forests, the need for animals to have a home, and the interconnectedness of all living things. It is also in this setting that children learn to appreciate the beauty and diversity of the natural world and how to relate to it in a respectful and caring way. They come to know themselves as a part of this world and, over time, discover a corresponding beauty and diversity in the world of humans.

Marti's backyard has been described by one of the parents as "a child's paradise" and "a world of imagination and make-believe with a purpose." Butterflies and hummingbirds flit about while classical music wafts overhead. Children and parents love this place, and find it a welcome refuge from the hectic world outside.

The Uniqueness of the Program

While the daily routine and structure of the Young Naturalist Center resemble, in many ways, any other developmentally appropriate early childhood program, there are some subtle but important differences. Aspects of the program where these differences are evident include "circle time," planning the learning environment, curricular content, nature of the outdoor area, and child-initiated play. "Circle time," in many programs, tends to emphasize the "time" over the "circle." Teachers in traditional programs usually announce "circle time" as a time for the children to set aside their own materials and activities and attend to a teacher-directed activity. "Circle time" at the Young Naturalist Center, on the other hand, means a "gathering together" in an environment where feelings are shared and positive social interaction is stressed.

There are also differences in the part of the program that is sometimes referred to as "room arrangement" or "planning the learning environment." In a typical preschool, room arrangement is decided by the teacher—in fact, a major part of the teacher's role is to "arrange the learning environment." At the Young Naturalist Center, the environment belongs to the children. The school is "their place"; and as long as the children respect the natural en-

vironment and each other, they are free to arrange the environment as they see fit.

Differences between the Young Naturalist Center and traditional preschools are also evident in the content of the curriculum. Traditional preschools tend to focus on growth in the different development domains (language development, physical development, cognitive development, social-emotional development, etc.) and the acquisition of pre-academic skills (pre-math, pre-reading, basic concepts relating to science and social studies, etc.). The primary focus of the Young Naturalist Center, however, is on understanding and caring for the natural environment, for each other, and for people of every culture.

In most preschools, children learn about safety. They learn this primarily through the message that getting hurt would be bad. At the Young Naturalist Center, children learn to respect and care for their body. They learn this primarily through the message that staying well is good.

The outdoor area in most preschools means a playground—a place equipped

with different types of playground equipment (swings, climbers, slides, etc.) The outdoor area at the Young Naturalist Center is a theater, an art studio, a forest, an orchard, and anything else the children want it to be.

Child-initiated play in most preschools starts with a planning session, when children address the question, "What would you like to do?" Child-initiated play at the Young Naturalist Center is more likely to start with a visualization activity, where children ponder the question, "What would you like to be?"

Comments from parents indicate that they chose the Young Naturalist Center for its philosophy and uniqueness. One mother said that she enrolled her son in the program precisely because it was different. "I didn't want a typical preschool with brightly colored playground equipment and plastic furniture. I wanted something more natural." Another parent commented on the natural environment: "As soon as I walked in and saw it, I knew this was the place for my son—a place where he could run and touch and feel and play—a place

to play in the bushes and sit in the grass. I had these things when I was a kid, and I want the same for him."

Plans, Activities, and Program Policies

Marti plans her daily lessons and activities around a variety of themes—all relating in some way to the natural environment and multicultural understandings. Young children learn primarily through play, and Marti's backyard is a perfect setting for stimulating active, imaginative play. It's easy to pretend that you're a howler monkey or a jaguar in a rainforest, when you're surrounded with trees to climb and bushes in which to hide.

Ancient stories, folktales, and legends play a major role in the program at the Young Naturalist Center. Marti carefully researches ancient myths and legends to identify the stories that can speak to the children about reverence for the natural environment and respect for the cultural heritage of our ancestors. Marti firmly believes that young children see the world through eyes very much like those of our ancient ancestors, who related to myths and legends long before the invention of the written word. Just as our ancestors sang their stories, danced them, and expressed them in paintings and carvings, so Marti involves the children in an exploration of the myths through a variety of activities and within a variety of environments. Marti encourages children to listen to the stories, not just with their ears, but with their hearts as well.

After sharing a legend orally with the children, Marti introduces a variety of dance and theater activities in which children have the opportunity to reenact the story at their level of understanding. After the reenactment, she then invites the children to tell the story again through their hands, as they work through the medium of arts and crafts. Utilizing the colors, shapes, and textures of natural objects and recyclable household articles, a child can conceptualize the characters and action of the story, depict it in a three-dimensional object, and then stand back and see that it is real.

There aren't many "toys" at the Young Naturalist Center. Children are encouraged to make their own. Many natural materials are provided as incentives for the toy-making process. Pieces of bark may be used for boats, leaves become plates on the tree stump tables, while sticks and stones serve as building blocks for constructing houses or dens.

Children at the Young Naturalist Center are often encouraged to work together. Even an art project becomes a collaborative effort. After listening to a story, the children are encouraged to draw a picture of what they liked about the story. Only one large sheet of paper is provided. One child draws a picture and talks about what he or she liked about the story. The paper and crayons are then passed to the next child and the next, until each child has had a turn to add to the picture. All the

children's names are printed on the paper and the picture is proudly hung near the front entrance for all to enjoy.

Disputes and disagreements between children are handled through words, not actions. With the help of the teachers, children learn to talk over their differences. No child is ever separated from the group for discipline purposes. The message to the children is that they are a part of a group and must learn to get along in that group. Gentleness and cooperation are deliberately taught, while violent behavior is never accepted. There aren't many "do's and don'ts" at the Young Naturalist Center; but understood by all is the rule about "No monsters, no guns or other weapons, and no hitting." When necessary, children are reminded that words, too, can be used as weapons but that this is not acceptable. Marti and Kathy (Marti's coteacher) remind the children to be gentle and caring toward each other. In talking with the children, they are likely to say, "We don't hurt any living thing and your friends are living, aren't they? We never use weapons of our hands or our mouths."

In addition to learning to live in harmony with each other, children are also taught to live in harmony with the natural environment. Children are taught not to do anything to harm the natural environment—thus, they avoid breaking branches from the trees, picking wild flowers, and disturbing the nests of birds and insects. The children are taught not to be wasteful—they may pick an apple or dig a carrot only if they plan to eat it. They use recycled materials in their arts and crafts projects, and are careful not to overuse paper, glue, water, and other consumable materials.

Role of the Teacher

The role of the teacher at the Young Naturalist Center is that of facilitator and guide, versus instructor. Marti and her co-teacher, Kathy, move about among the children as they play. They make comments and ask questions, but always with care, so as not to direct or intrude. Through their words and actions, they gently extend the children's learning and understandings. Typical questions relate to what the children are doing and experiencing: "Who are you building the shelter for?" "If you're going to be the medicine man, what do you think you might need?" The teachers may also introduce a special prop to enhance dramatic play. A blue cloth might be offered to help define a "pond," or a backpack to make the "hiking" experience more realistic.

Teachers introduce new vocabulary and concepts, but always in the context of what the children are doing. If the children have taken on the role of large animals in the forest, Marti might become one of them and say, "We have to creep, stalk, move quickly and quietly to catch the bugs out of the air."

Teachers also respond positively to what the children say and do. When a child yells that an animal puppet is eating his hand, Marti responds by saying, "Maybe you could ask him to let you go." If children seem "stuck" in their play, a suggestion from Marti or Kathy will usually rekindle their interest. "Maybe you could help the frog find a place to live. If you dig a hole in the sand, I'll get some water."

Summary

The Young Naturalist Center provides a unique program combining early childhood education, environmental education, and multicultural education. A large part of the curriculum is built around myths and stories from various cultures and from ideas shared by families about their own cultures and customs. The program is designed to infuse in young children attitudes of respect for the diversity inherent in natural and social environments and to foster ways of living in harmony with both.

Fairgreen Nursery School
Joyce Davis

Section Overview

The Fairgreen Parent Cooperative Nursery School in Toledo, Ohio, was founded in 1972 by Joyce Davis, who still serves as the early childhood administrator. Through the years, with the cooperation and teamwork of teachers and parents working together, a nature-based curriculum was developed. This curriculum reflects a holistic approach to early childhood education and incorporates puppets, music, art, nutritious snacks, literature, and creative movement. The preschool is housed in a Presbyterian Church. The following program description was written by Joyce Davis, who likes to describe her curriculum in terms of an ongoing "celebration."

The content of the curriculum at Fairgreen Nursery School is nature based and focuses on celebrations. Everything that the children do, learn, and care for is celebrated (i.e., surrounded with festivity). Childhood itself is viewed as a celebration. This view is expressed through positive words and behaviors and through a "fun approach" to learning.

Learning and caring about the natural world's fragile existence are also emphasized throughout the various aspects of the curriculum. Each day is a celebration as children and adults encounter an insect, seed, animal, or rainbow. The school year starts with children and adults experiencing September through nature's gifts. While some monarch caterpillars munch on milk-weed children have gathered, others are in their chrysalis in various stages preparing to emerge as butterflies. They will soon be fed sugar water, with young children observing the proboscis as they drink. These beautiful orange-black beauties will then be released to fly to Mexico for the winter.

Throughout the month of September, the children applaud the cycles of butterflies, moths, and ladybugs. They come to know that the coddling moth caterpillar feeds inside the apple; and that it is actually a caterpillar in an ear of corn—not a worm! September's experiences and gifts of nature foster an enrichment of language, an understanding of other places and cultures, and an appreciation of the natural world.

Puppets—in the form of animal characters—play a major role in the Fairgreen preschool classroom. They are an integral part of the daily activities and help teachers motivate children to listen, remember, and respect insects, animals, trees, plants, and Planet Earth. The puppets dress for the theme of the day and challenge the children to wonder and discover as they present "gifts of nature." An ear of corn is one example of a gift of nature. The puppets talk to the children about the "friends of corn" that helped those delicious seeds mature for our eating pleasure. The puppets may also give some corn seeds to the children for planting.

Children and adults actively listen as a puppet relates facts and introduces new vocabulary and concepts about some aspect of nature. They then engage in a variety of hands-on activities related to what the puppet has introduced. They might prepare and taste a "related" snack, or become involved with songs, books, creative movement and drama relating to the theme of the day. They also spend time in a "natural area" outdoors where they discover and become comfortable with many aspects of nature. They find ways to celebrate a cricket, acorn, pumpkin or a swallowtail caterpillar. They might paint with Queen Anne's lace, a favorite food of the swallowtail.

Nature lends itself well to a developmentally appropriate curriculum. It offers innumerable opportunities for hands-on experiences and invites children's active exploration. The Fairgreen Nursery School taps into these positive characteristics of the natural environment and provides a program that fosters an understanding and appreciation of the world of nature. Care is also taken to ensure that the experiences provided are multicultural, nonsexist, and attentive to individual needs and interests. Such a program helps children grow up wanting to be more than Ninja Turtles and Ghost Busters. They want to be archaeologists, paleontologists, farmers, scientists, nurses, teachers, firefighters, etc. Hopefully, they will also be environmentalists and protectors of the natural environment.

Life Cycle Projects
Linda Penn*

"The power of the presence" might be an adequate description for the impact of living things in the preschool learning environment. The butterfly life cycle presents one of the most persuasive examples of this power of the presence. The butterfly cycle has a tendency to teach paradoxically—from provoking intense interest and excitement, all the way to engendering patience, tenderness, and respect—as quiet observation and gentle caretaking allow a sharing in the wonder of complete metamorphosis.

It is interesting to notice that young children can have an even more profound sharing in nature's life cycles than the adults who enthusiastically provide the learning opportunity. Being diminutive has a definite advantage in this instance, as children seem to possess a special understanding and empathy for "little" living things. They themselves are so much smaller than the adult world that surrounds and supports them; thus, experiencing a life cycle permits the young person to be the nurturing adult in Lilliputian land.

It can truly be said, especially in reference to young children, that **life cycle experiences present nature close-up**. A butterfly life cycle, for example, can place children close to the earth physically and emotionally. Watching a tiny egg hatch into a caterpillar and then into a butterfly allows children to experience the dramatic event of changing from a flower of the earth to a jewel of the sky, taking flight on "wings of wonder" in the form of a butterfly! Experiencing life cycle events with preschoolers reminds one of the real human need to celebrate the magic of life and the rhythms of nature.

*Linda's celebrations are often expressed through musical compositions. Her interest in composing nature-related songs started with her own children's attempts to express the wonders of nature through music. They were "silly songs" at first, but soon turned into prayers for a Sunday School Program. From there, Linda moved on to developing a series of SING-ALONG SCIENCE SONGS, often used with young children to celebrate the wonders of life.

Fe y Algería
Adelia Peters, Ph.D.

Section Overview

Described in this section is an alternative community-based educational program originally developed for children in Latin America. This program, Fe y Algería, has become an important part of many early childhood programs. The author of this section, Dr. Adelia Peters, sees Fe y Algería as having the potential for introducing or expanding environmental education to a large population of young children.

With the passage of the North American Free Trade Agreement (NAFTA), educators in the United States may be drawn to examine some innovative, alternative educational programs in Latin America. The introduction of young children to the natural world and the integration of learning experiences in nature with day care and preschool programs fit well with the philosophy of a widespread set of programs known as Fey Alegría.

Fey Alegría (Faith and Joy) is a nongovernmental organization designed to provide formal as well as nonformal education at different levels in 12 Latin American countries. The organization began in 1955 as a project of Fr. José M. V alaz, of Caracas, to help provide quality education to poor children. "Where the asphalt road ends, where there is no water, electricity, or services, there begins Fey Alegría" serves as the motto of the groups involved (Reimers, 1993).

By 1992 the program had expanded to 509 centers among the 12 countries, and now reaches more than 500,000 people. The fastest growing segments of Fey Alegría are the day care and preschool programs. As of 1991 more than 42,000 participants were in day care or preschool programs. The preschool enrollments alone expanded 46% between 1990 and 1991, reflecting substantial growth, particularly in Brazil (Reimers, 1993).

According to a group of Latin American educators and journalists the author spoke with recently, Fey Alegría's schools and programs provide excellent opportunities for the development of environmental education for young children. There is an increasing emphasis in many Latin American countries upon educating the next generation to value and preserve the natural world. Workshops for Project Learning Tree, for example, were provided for more than 180 teachers in Brazil's state of Santa Catarina within a six-month period in 1992-93. Another example of the changing, more positive views in Latin America regarding the environment is the rapid development of eco-tourism. In Costa Rica, when the prices of bananas and coffee fell, eco-tourism provided an important source of foreign currency. Introducing young children to the wonders of nature seems a logical outgrowth of the emphasis in Latin America upon movements such as eco-tourism. The next generation will play a vital role in the development of values related to the environment.

Early childhood educators in the United States might be inspired by the successful experiences of Fe y Algería, especially with children from rural and urban areas where poverty is high. Some of the key goals and policies of the organization are described below.

As with many environmental education programs, Fe y Alegría leaders seek to create active partnerships among the organization's leaders, the state, and the local communities to improve and enhance the educational opportunities for children living in poverty. In the formal educational settings, the Ministry of Education often pays the salaries of the teachers while the community members take care of the construction and maintenance of the schools and programs. Often schools operate as centers for community development. Among the programs that have proven successful are health and food programs and programs to support the leaders of the organizations of mothers. Mothers, especially, are becoming more actively involved in the development of improved, more equitable educational opportunities for the children who are the next generation. Establishing a community of parents remains an important part of all schools in Fey Alegría.

In Bolivia in 1992, Fe y Alegría developed boarding schools as alternative models for rural education. Called "Houses of Knowledge," they have their own school governments, and students participate in establishing community rules and electing boards to maintain discipline. Community members participate by bringing food and supplies, and local mothers assist with food preparation. Students keep school gardens and cultivate fruits and vegetables. No mention is made of the ages of the students.

Although Fe y Alegría programs provide education for a relatively small percentage of all children enrolled in school in each country (less than three in one thousand primary school children), one might view them as yeast for the larger public school systems. The programs are most developed in Bolivia, where three of every one

hundred children in primary school attend a Fey Alegría school.

Among the specific goals of the Fey Alegría movement that could contribute to establishing a good learning climate for early childhood environmental education are

- Education emphasizing learning processes and content that originate in the reality of the daily life of the child

- An active, critical, and creative pedagogy

- Education in productive work

- Education that confronts community problems

- Education in participation

- Education that fosters a permanent learning process

- Education committed to a new model of humanity and society (Fey Alegría, 1992)

Fe y Alegría has the goal of education in Christian values, also. (Although it is an institution of the Roman Catholic Church, in 1991 only 6% of the teachers and principals were members of a religious congregation.) In Bolivia the emphasis is placed upon education that provides a transcendent dimension to motivate individuals throughout life.

As more Latin American countries seek to govern through democracies, child-centered, active, participatory education efforts may increase. The emphasis in Fe y Alegría's programs upon "learning processes and content that originate in the reality of daily life" is in contrast to the emphasis in many public schools in Latin America on rote learning, using materials that are far removed from the life of the child growing up in poverty. Although most of the goals listed in Fe y Alegría lend themselves to the inclusion of environmental education in many age groups, the potential is especially great for introducing environmental education in the early childhood years.

The close integration of the educational programs of Fe y Alegría with other activities of the community is considered to be one of the organization's greatest strengths. In the view of FernandoReimers (1993), schools in Latin America often have hidden curricula that teach apathy, hopelessness, resignation, and acceptance of social class disparities. Children wait for the central government to solve problems. The implementation of the goals of Fe y Alegría may lead to a generation of children who actively support the preservation and conservation of the natural world.

References

Fe y Alegría. (1992). Propuesta Educativa de Fe y Alegría, Calidid de la Educacion. Caraca, Venezuela. Quoted in Reimers, F., 1993, pp. 14, 34.

Reimers, F. (1993). <u>Education and the consolidation of democracy in Latin America: Innovations to provide quality basic education with equity</u>. Advocacy Series: Education and Development. Cambridge: Harvard Institute for International Development.

"Learning Together" Programs
Kelly J. Warren

Section Overview

The early childhood environmental education program described in this section is unique in that it serves adults and children together. This section was written by Kelly Warren, who develops and leads "Learning Together" programs at the University of Wisconsin-Arboretum.

Children's basic attitudes towards life, their approach to new experiences, and their feelings about themselves and others are established in the first few years of life. Children's attitudes towards the natural environment are forming then as well. Increasing environmental awareness at an early age tends to build a secure foundation for further discovery, inquiry, and knowledge of one's surroundings. This awareness can remain with children through their years of schooling and into adulthood, enabling them to make prudent, responsible decisions about their effect on the natural world.

"Learning Together" programs were designed to enhance young children's understanding and appreciation of the natural environment. These programs offer a unique approach to environmental education in that, as the title implies, both preschooler and adult learn about the natural environment. In order for this to occur, activities are designed to address the intellectual levels of both young children and adults. For example, a Sensory Walk through the prairie would include color searches and texture and shape hunts for the child, while providing information to the adult about the prairie's natural history and how to identify different types of plants, insects, and birds. Because attention is paid to the interests of parents and children, both groups are more willing to explore and stay involved.

"Learning Together" programs have recently been developed at the University of Wisconsin-Arboretum. These programs were developed in response to the adult's interest in the child's learning and enjoyment of the natural world as well as the adult's desire to be an intricate part of the experience. The adult may be a parent, an older sibling, grandparent, aunt, uncle, or godparent. Name tags identify adults as "Great Aunt Margaret," "Grandpa Frank," "Aunt Nancy," etc.

The first "Learning Together" program at the University of Wisconsin-Arboretum focused on communities, with a different community highlighted each session. Communities addressed were pond, prairie, and woodland. The focus of each session was refined even further by targeting a specific class of animal living in the designated habitat. On the woodland day, for example, we focused on the soil community and the creatures living there.

The activities for this day started out with a Soil Sort. Adults and children gathered around a pile of soil and began to sort, into egg cartons, the five components of soil: plants (dead and alive), animals (dead and alive), rocks (large to small), air, and water. For the water component, we grabbed a handful of soil and squeezed out the water. For the air, we scooped up an armful and placed it in the egg carton. We made a point of "stocking" insects for the group to discover during this activity.

After the Soil Sort, we made "soil insect" necklaces. Images of common insects such as sowbug, millipede, centipede, ant, slug, and earthworm (not an insect, but likely to be found) were carved out of erasers and mounted on a block of wood to be used as stamps. The children used these stamps on small, precut cards and, with the help of the adults, wrote the corresponding name of the insect on each of the cards. These cards were then laced on a string (piece of yarn) and formed into a necklace shape.

With necklaces adorned, we went on an insect hunt in the woods, turning over rocks and logs to search for the animals in their real habitat. Later, we used puppets to tell stories about other animals who live in the woods and who may meet the insects that were introduced earlier. These "other animals" included the mole, skunk, squirrel, and toad.

The overall evaluations of this initial session was quite positive. Many adults stated that they would like to see a year-round "Learning Together" program. One main criticism (that we all felt) was that individual groups were too large (12-16 people per group). During the next two sessions, many children returned with their grandfathers, aunts, or older sibling, in addition to the adult who participated in the first session. They all left knowing a little more about insects that inhabit the woodlands, and that was our primary goal.

The staff at the University of Wisconsin-Arboretum learned several lessons from these initial "Learning Together" sessions. They found that they must keep a very narrow focus when working with three- to five-year-old children, and that the planned activities must clearly relate to the narrowly defined theme. Next year the Arboretum plans to expand the "Learning Together" program threefold. The size of each group will be limited by staffing more naturalists each session. Confidence is running high in anticipation of another successful year with the "Learning Together" program.

Beyond Our Wildest Dreams!
Eleanor W. Tinto

About three years ago, several experienced volunteers at the Louisiana Nature and Science Center (LNSC)—Lavergne Backes, a retired teacher and preschool principal; Barbara Schneider, a retired teacher; and Eleanor Tinto, a retired teacher—recognized a grave need for environmental involvement at the crucial preschool age. A natural outgrowth of this was the "Preschool Program" that was developed for the LNSC in New Orleans. This program was designed for children in day care groups, in recognition of the fact that the era of the "stay-at-home mom" (who can interact with her child, nature, and the LNSC) has passed. The overall purpose of the program is to introduce nature and the mission of the LNSC (which is environmental education) to children in day care programs.

The curriculum for this program is designed to instill awareness in young children of their role in all aspects of the balance of nature and to further stimulate this awareness through positive interactions within the natural environment. The response to this curriculum indicates that children of preschool age are very accepting of nature-related concepts as diverse as whales, snails, and recycling.

Originally planned were two sessions of one hour each, to be held one Wednesday of the month for eight months during the school year. A monthly topic (based on scientifically accurate material) would be repeated biannually (thus there would be a total of 16 topics). This program proved successful beyond our wildest dreams! The program has now expanded to offering sessions three Wednesdays per month for eight months.

But ask now the beasts,
and they shall teach thee;
and the fowls of the air,
and they shall teach thee;
or speak to the earth,
and it shall teach thee;
and the fishes of the sea
shall declare unto thee.

Job 12:7-8

Epilogue: Hope for the Future
Ruth A. Wilson, Ph.D.

Children today are growing up in a society that values owning and controlling, where the natural world is viewed as an unlimited resource for humankind, and where many children have infrequent opportunities for positive interactions with the natural environment. Such a society does not teach understanding and appreciation of the natural environment, nor does it teach children that the Earth is a community to which they belong.

It is, without doubt, time to structure society around a new vision of what our world ought to be. Passing the world on to our children in the condition that it is—full of war and violence, neglect and misuse—would certainly be a tragedy and an injustice. We need to let our children know that peace and caring and a responsible way of relating to the Earth are possible.

Environmental education can be the vehicle for sharing this message with our children, but the time to start is during the early childhood years. If children fail to develop an interest in and an appreciation of the natural world while they are still very young, they are at risk of never developing positive and caring attitudes toward the world of nature. If we want a new world vision to become reality, we must be willing and insightful enough to invest in quality environmental education for our very young children—for they are our hope for the future.

Ideas on how to structure a new way of living, more in harmony with the natural world, might be gathered from a study of the Native American practice of the Vision Quest. The Vision Quest was undertaken by Native Americans as an odyssey of self-knowledge and fulfillment. It was a spiritual journey into the wilderness and the soul. The Vision Quest experience required time alone in the wilderness—a time for reflecting and growing in wisdom and understanding. Individuals on a Vision Quest did not study books nor did they conduct scientific investigations. They were looking for—and often found—a different way of knowing. Their sermons were delivered in the wind; their songs and chants were carried by the birds and bubbling brooks; their spiritual guides were the animals who gradually revealed themselves to the individuals seeking guidance and understanding. The Vision Quest often brought about a metamorphosis of the spirit and with it peace, insight, and a sense of well-being.

Perhaps a metamorphosis of the human spirit is what is needed to ensure a future for our children, our society, and our world. Needed changes include a move from wanting more money, power, and material things to valuing simplicity and ingenuity. It requires a move from a throw-away society to a reuse and recycle society. It requires a move from manicuring lawns to planting gardens. It means less time spent at malls and amusement parks and more time in the woods and along the streams. It means fewer swimming pools, and cleaner oceans and lakes. It means a move away from one-person cars, which isolate us from each other and pollute the environment, to more carpooling and public transportation options. It means less demand for exotic and out-of-season foods to an appreciation of home-grown and locally produced foods.

Changes are also needed in how we educate our children. It's time for our pursuit of knowledge to focus more on the whole and on interconnections than on individual parts and classifications. It's time for less "busy work" in our schools and more meaningful involvement in community projects. It's time for educational programs to focus on learning how to learn, learning how to ask good questions, and being open to and evaluating new concepts. It's time to focus on context in our educational programs instead of content and the acquisition of a prescribed bank of information. It's time to view learning as a process or journey, versus a product or destination. It's time to introduce a different type of learning environment—one that takes into consideration such factors as aesthetics, physical comfort, and the need for both privacy and interaction. School environments should be planned to accommodate both quiet and exuberant activities versus being designed for efficiency and convenience. It's time to move away from an overemphasis on "book knowledge" to a recognition of the value of hands-on experiences both in and out of the classroom. Schools need to spend more time, money, and energy in planning their outdoor learning environments and should make field trips and internships a regular and valued part of each student's learning experience.

It's exciting and humbling to know that we can be the people of transition. We can and must be the ones with vision for the future. If we keep things the way they are and continually walk down the path of use and misuse, the path will soon become a rut. Once a rut gets to a certain depth, people walking along that path can no longer see anything but the walls around them. Perhaps we haven't dug that deeply yet. Perhaps we can still envision a bigger and more beautiful world. As people of transition, we need to crawl out of the rut and walk a new path.

Let's lead our children down this new path. Let's teach them to appreciate the beauty and mystery of the natural world. Let's teach them about gardening and recycling. Let's get them involved in meaningful projects, and let's get the community involved with the schools. Let's define our curriculum by vision instead of goals. Let's move beyond motivating children to inspiring them. Let's encourage our children to reflect, ponder, question, dream, plan, fail, succeed, rethink, invent, and imagine. Let's teach our children not only to sing songs, but to hear the songs within themselves. Let's teach our children not only to dance, but to dance in harmony with the universe.

Let's help our children discover the spiritual connection that exists between their souls and the natural world. Once they discover this connection, they'll know that when they deface the Earth, they deface their souls as well. They'll know that if they destroy all the wild places on Earth, they'll destroy their avenue for creativity and enthusiasm for life.

Our best bet for saving the natural environment rests with the very young. They're the ones who haven't yet built up prejudices against the world of nature. They can still fall in love with the natural environment. Let's foster this love affair by giving them frequent opportunities to take walks in the woods and the meadows, to collect shells along a sandy beach, to sleep outdoors on a starry night, and to grow flowers and tomatoes in gardens of their own. Let's show them how to gently stroke the moss on the side of a tree, to stand quietly in a wooded area and listen to the birds and the rustling of leaves, to sit beside a bubbling stream and watch the sunlight make diamonds in the water.

Let's also foster this love affair by giving teachers opportunities to grow in wisdom and love for the Earth. Let's provide wilderness retreats for teachers—especially teachers of the very young. And let's turn to the words of Walt Whitman for guidance on how to raise wise and peaceful people: "Now I see the secret of the making of the best persons. It is to grow in the open air, and to eat and sleep with the earth."

Appendix

In the fall of 1991, an informal network was created to promote environmental education at the early childhood level. This network is based on the assumption that if environmental education is to be optimally effective, it must start at the early childhood level (Carson, 1956; Disinger, 1985/86; Iozzi, 1989; Wilson, 1993). The current mailing list for the network numbers over 1000 and includes individuals from more than 40 different countries.

Rationale for the International Network

"Environmental Education for Preschoolers" is based on the understanding that the underlying causes of contemporary environmental problems are closely linked to behavior patterns and value systems of individuals who consume and sometimes misuse natural resources. The restoration and future protection of the environment depend, to a great extent, on the development of an environmental ethic. Changes in attitudes, values, and behaviors are critically important at this time in history, for survival.

The network is designed to provide members with opportunities to share information regarding resource materials, conferences, workshops, organizations related to early childhood environmental education, and research activities and results; above all, it encourages an active support group for environmental education at the preschool level. Multicultural perspectives are encouraged as having great potential for enhancing awareness and appreciation of both the natural environmental and the human community.

Attitudes toward the natural environment influence the way people think, feel, and act toward their surroundings. Changing the attitudes and behaviors of people toward the natural environment is recognized as one of the greatest challenges facing education in the future (Baker, 1983; Shane, 1989; Willis, 1989). A review of the professional literature suggests that positive experiences related to the out-of-doors during a child's preschool years have the potential for influencing lifelong attitudes and behaviors toward the natural environment (Carson, 1956; Iozzi, 1989; Tokar, 1987).

Networking Activities

Among the activities promoted since 1991 are

- Providing opportunities for professional development in early childhood environmental education (ECEE)
- Planning and conducting meetings, sometimes in conjunction with professional conferences (e.g., a preconference workshop at the annual conference of the Ohio Association for the Education of Young Children)
- Developing and disseminating a newsletter supporting ECEE, the Earthworm (Spring, 1993, one issue)
- Networking with other groups involved in environmental education, multicultural education, and early childhood education
- Sharing and expanding resources and ideas for fostering positive environmental attitudes in young children (e.g., establishing and providing information about a lending library of materials for ECEE at Bowling Green State University, Bowling Green, Ohio)
- Writing and disseminating a curriculum guide for ECEE: Fostering a Sense of

<u>Wonder during the Early Childhood Years</u>, by Ruth Wilson

- Providing workshops and seminars for teacher training
- Fostering research and program evaluation in ECEE
- Establishing a mailing list, including international participants from more than 40 countries

The organizers of the network are actively pursuing other opportunities, including e-mail, to link with existing groups in early childhood education and environmental education.

Membership Information

If you are not a member of the network but would like to be, photocopy and complete the "Needs and Information Survey." Mail or Fax it to RuthWilson at the address on the form.

For more information or additional copies of the survey contact one of us.

Dr. Ruth Wilson, Associate Professor
Department of Special Education
Bowling Green State University
Bowling Green, OH 43403 USA
Tel. 419/372-7278
Fax 419/372-8265
email: rwilso2@andy.bgsu.edu

Dr. Adelia Peters, Professor
Educational Foundations and Inquiry
Bowling Green State University
Bowling Green, OH 43403 USA
Tel. 419/372-7339
Fax 419/372-8265
email: apeters@andy.bgsu.edu

References

Baker, C. (1983). Evaluation and accountability. <u>Journal of Physical Education, Recreation, and Dance, 54</u> (1), 58-59.

Carson, R. (1956). <u>The sense of wonder</u>. New York: Harper & Row.

Disinger, J. F. (1985/86). Current trends in environmental education. <u>Journal of Environmental Education, 17</u> (2), 1-3.

Iozzi, L.A. (1989). What research says to the educator. Part Two: Environmental education and the affective domain. <u>Journal of Environmental Education, 20</u>, (4), 6-13.

Shane, H. G. (1989, September). Educated foresight for the 1990's. <u>Educational Leadership</u>, pp. 4-6.

Tokar, B. (1987). <u>The green alternative</u>. San Pedro: R. & E. Miles.

Willis, S. (1989, September). On education for alternative futures: A conversation with Sam Keen. <u>Educational Leadership</u>, pp. 73-75.

Wilson, R. A. (1993). <u>Fostering a sense of wonder during the early childhood years</u>. Columbus, OH: Greyden Press.

"Environmental Education for Preschoolers" Network
Needs and Information Survey

BACKGROUND INFORMATION

Name _____

Address (Check preferred mailing address. Home_____, Business_____):

    Home _____
                _____

    Business _____
                _____

Phone: Home _____ Office _____ Fax: _____

E-Mail Address _____ Business Affiliation _____

Present Position _____ No. of years in position _____

Education:

Highest earned degree	Major area of emphasis (if appropriate)
____ Primary school	
____ Secondary school	
____ Associate degree (junior or community college)	_____
____ Undergraduate (B.A./B.S. degree)	_____
____ Graduate (post graduate) degree	
____ Master's	_____
____ Specialist	_____
____ Doctorate	_____

Teaching certificate(s):

Certification areas	Age levels
_____	_____
_____	_____
_____	_____

Other educational certificates/licenses/diplomas, etc.	Conferring agency/institution
_____	_____

Other experiences related to environmental education/early childhood education: List previous positions held. Circle the area(s) most descriptive of those position(s). (EE = environmental education; EC = early childhood education; ECEE = early childhood environmental education)

Positions held

_____ EE   EC   ECEE

_____ EE   EC   ECEE

_____ EE   EC   ECEE

Organizations or groups you think might welcome a link with early childhood environmental education. Indicate whether or not you are a member.

Professional organizations   Check if you are a member

_____   _____

_____   _____

_____   _____

_____   _____

Government/nongovernment/civic/
community organizations   Check if you are a member

_____   _____

_____   _____

_____   _____

_____   _____

Current support services/resources
Please list any newsletters or journals you currently use to support your early childhood environmental education ECEE activities.

_____   _____

_____   _____

Please list any networks (associations, e-mail, electronic bulletin boards, etc.) that currently support your ECEE activities.

_____   _____

_____   _____

Please list any other resources (e.g., ERIC Clearinghouse) you currently use for your ECEE activities.

_____   _____

_____   _____

NEEDS ASSESSMENT

This section focuses on _information and networking needs_ related to early childhood environmental education. Indicate, by circling the appropriate number below, the relative importance of each item to you.

<u>Level of importance</u>
(5 = high; 1 = low; N = not important)

	Level of importance
Newsletters/journals	5 4 3 2 1 N
continue <u>Earthworm</u> newsletter	5 4 3 2 1 N
Curriculum resources	5 4 3 2 1 N
Research activities/results	5 4 3 2 1 N
Conference/meeting information	5 4 3 2 1 N
Educational opportunities (workshops, seminars, courses)	
academic credit	5 4 3 2 1 N
noncredit	5 4 3 2 1 N
Other (please list)	
_____	5 4 3 2 1 N
_____	5 4 3 2 1 N

<u>Priorities for strengthening ECEE</u>

Establish a new organization, including a newsletter (estimated cost $20 to $30)	5 4 3 2 1 N
Increase focus of ECEE in existing organizations	5 4 3 2 1 N

Other suggestions for meeting ECEE
information and/or networking needs:

_____	5 4 3 2 1
_____	5 4 3 2 1

Names and addresses of others who may be interested in ECEE:

_____

_____

_____

Other comments:

_____

_____

_____

_____

Please return completed surveys as soon as possible to
    Dr. Ruth Wilson
    Department of Special Education
    Bowling Green State University
    Bowling Green, OH 43403 USA
    Fax: 419/372-8265

ENVIRONMENTAL EDUCATION FOR PRESCHOOLERS

Selected Resources

An Early Start to Nature. R. Richards. New York: Simon & Schuster, 1989.

Provides information and activities concerning trees, plants, birds, invertebrates, water life, and the moon and stars. Emphasis is placed on the child's practical investigation at first hand.

Animals in the Classroom. D. Kramer. New York: Addison-Wesley, 1989.

Sourcebook for teachers interested in keeping a variety of small animals in the classroom—earthworms, snails, crickets, hermit crabs, frogs, hamsters, birds—28 animals covered in all. For each, this book explains natural history, how to obtain, housing and diet, observations and activities, and what to do when the project is over.

Bridging Early Childhood and Nature Education. Jamestown, NY: Roger Tory Peterson Institute, 1991.

Report begins with an overview of Roger Peterson's recollections of childhood experiences that influenced his development as a naturalist; it affirms the value of nature education for young children and offers basic reference questions, a discussion of developmental appropriateness, and guidelines for selecting activities for young children.

Earth Child. K. Sheehan & M. Waidner. Tulsa, OK: Council Oak Books, 1991.

This activity book includes exercises, games, stories, and songs to be shared by children and adults. It also includes many ecology-related resources for adults and annotated lists of children's nature books. Topics cover the role of the sun, earth celebrations, habitats, compassion for animals, endangered species, and peace-keeping practices. Goals of the activities include nurturing imagination, empathy, and a deeper understanding of the earth, and teaching conservation and the interconnectedness of all living things.

Fostering a Sense of Wonder during the Early Childhood Years. R. A. Wilson. Columbus, OH: Greyden Press, 1993.

A curriculum guide designed to infuse environmental education into all aspects of an early childhood program.

Good Earth Art: Environmental Art for Kids. M.Kohl & C. Gainer. Bellingham, WA: Bright Ring Publishing, 1991.

Over 200 activities use recycled and natural materials and teach environmental responsibility. Each activity is coded for type of material, age range, group or individual project, and special safety concerns. Collages, weaving, printmaking, wood-scrap sculpture, and painting activities are new routes to understanding both science and nature.

Hands-on Nature: Information and Activities for Exploring the Environment with Children. J.Lingelbach (editor). Woodstock, VT: Vermont Institute of Natural Science, 1986.

Nature "workshops" are grouped into four separate chapters: Adaptations, Habitats, Cycles, and Designs of Nature. Within the chapters, the workshops are arranged in seasonal order. Within each workshop there are two main parts: an informational essay, which includes resources, and an activity section. Grades K-6.

Hug a Tree and Other Things to Do Outdoors with Young Children. R. Rockwell, E. Sherwood, &R.W illiams. Mt. Rainier, MD: Gryphon House, 1986.

This activity book provides 40 experiences for young children to have with nature. Activities focus on aesthetic and affective experiences, observation experiences, data collecting, measurement experiences, and watching time and seasons. The authors provide information regarding ways to organize the outdoor experience and reference books for parents, teachers, and children.

Kid's Gardening. L. Ocone & E. Pranis. Burlington, VT: National Gardening Association, 1990.

Provides information regarding the planning, development, and design of a garden for young people. Also provides activities and basics of indoor and outdoor gardening.

<u>Love the Earth: Exploring Environmental Activities for Young Children</u>. P. Claycomb. Livonia, MI: Partner Press, 1991.

Offers both indoor and outdoor activities that focus on similar concepts, such as insects, weather, animals, colors, and plants, plus a variety of related songs and fingerplays.

<u>Marmalade Days</u>. C. Taylor-Bond. Livonia, MI: Partner Press, 1987.

Provides the preschool and kindergarten teacher with complete learning units. Included are activities for each subject, directions, ready-made worksheets, patterns, and pictures of finished projects, words and actions of fingerplays and action songs, tunes or music for songs, recipes, and letters to parents.

<u>More Mudpies to Magnets</u>. E. Sherwood, R. Williams, & R. Rockwell. Mt. Rainier, MD: Gryphon House, 1990.

This curriculum guide includes 126 hands-on science experiments and activities. The instructions are clear and the results will hold the attention and excite the imagination of children ages 2-6. Science skills developed by the activities in the book include classification, measuring, using space and time relationships, communication, predicting and inferring, and numbers. Each activity outlines new words, equipment required, procedural steps, and enrichment ideas.

<u>Mudpies to Magnets</u>. E. Sherwood, R. Williams, & R. Rockwell. Mt. Rainier, MD: Gryphon House, 1987.

This book presents a science curriculum based on the natural curiosity of children. Eight curriculum units contain 112 hands-on activities for ages 2-5. Each activity outlines new words, equipment required, procedural steps, and enrichment ideas. Also includes tips on safety and planning and setting up a science activity center.

<u>My First Nature Book</u>. A. Wilkes. New York: Alfred A. Knopf, 1990.

A book written for children that provides indoor and outdoor nature activities. Simple and step-by-step instructions are given, as well as descriptions of the equipment needed and life-size photographs of the finished projects. Activities include making a terrarium, bird feeder, caterpillar house, and worm farm.

<u>Nature for the Very Young</u>. M. Bowden. New York: John Wiley & Sons, 1989.

This handbook of activities offers a combination of preschool readiness material and learning activities that use nature exploration as a springboard for learning and growing. Lessons are built around background information for the adults and proven learning activities for the children. The material is designed to focus on the basic concepts appropriate to a young child's level of development and ability. These concepts include color recognition, sequencing, body awareness, and reading readiness. Readers will also find guidance on leading a group of young children on field trips.

<u>Naturewatch: Exploring Nature with Your Children</u>. A. Katz. Menlo Park, CA: Addison-Wesley, 1986.

Offers parents, teachers, and children ways to explore and learn from the natural environment. Over 50 projects in the book require no special equipment or skills. With help from an adult, children will be able to tell the age of a tree or how to catch a spider's web intact. After learning to identify certain plants, each child will be ready to create a garden of his or her own, indoors or outdoors. A section on nature crafts shows how to create treasures from materials found in nature.

<u>Open the Door, Let's Explore</u>. R. Redleaf. Mt. Rainier, MD: Gryphon House, 1983.

This book contains ideas and activities associated with various field trips. Each trip lists several purposes one might consider for that trip, as well as vocabulary words that the children can learn as part of the experience. Included with each trip are original fingerplays and songs; selected books of fingerplays, songs, and general resource books are listed in an annotated bibliography.

<u>The Sense of Wonder</u>. R. Carson. Berkeley, CA: Harper & Row, 1956.

This book provides the magic and beauty that is all about us in the natural world. Bright-colored photos accompany and interpret Carson's words. Parents, children, and anyone who values natural beauty will treasure this reading experience.

Contributors

Eve Ameer is director of Children's Programs at the New Canaan Nature Center in New Canaan, Connecticut. She has a master of science degree in Speech Pathology and Audiology from Douglas College and has done postgraduate work at Rutgers University in Developmental Psychology. She has over 12 years of experience in teaching and administrating programs for young children.

Dona Greene Bolton is a teacher at the Child Development Center, a laboratory school for the Kent State College of Education, Kent, Ohio. In addition to teaching the nursery school classes, she also teaches a special five-week outdoor education program for four- to six-year-olds and an outdoor education summer workshop for returning teachers and graduate students. Ms.Bolton has traveled widely, studying early childhood and environmental education in various countries. She holds a master's degree in Children's Literature, and gives numerous workshops and presentations combining science and literature from a multicultural perspective. Ms. Bolton serves on the state board of the Ohio Association for the Study of Cooperation in Education and the board of trustees of several local environmental groups.

Richard Cohen is director of the Research Center at Pacific Oaks College in Pasadena, California. He holds a Ph.D. in Education from UCLA and an Ed.M. from the Harvard School of Education. Dr. Cohen has experience as a preschool teacher and has background in education evaluation and teacher education. He is coauthor of <u>Snail Trails and Tadpole Tails: Nature Education for Young Children</u>.

Stewart Cohen is professor of Human Development and Family Studies at the University of Rhode Island in Kingston, Rhode Island. Among his research interests is the study of places and settings including ecological awareness and correlative behavior in young children.

Joyce Davis is the founder and early childhood administrator for the Fairgreen Nursery School, which has been offering a nature-based program for over 20 years. Ms. Davis also makes puppets and video tapes that demonstrate the use of puppets in an early childhood classroom. Her puppet collection presently consists of about 30 different characters, including Sylvia the Spider, Lady Bug, Snail, Molting Caterpillar, Bullfrog, Turtle, Bee, and Rex the Rat. For more information about the puppets and video tapes contact "Joyce Davis -n- Puppets," 4025 Laskey Road, Toledo, OH 43623.

Jann Frisk is an early childhood special education teacher at Hope School in McClure, Ohio. She also worked as a research assistant at Bowling Green State University where she assisted in the development of <u>Fostering a Sense of Wonder during the Early Childhood Years</u>, an early childhood environmental education curriculum guide. Ms. Frisk has a master's degree in Early Childhood Special Education and is actively involved in developing a nature-based curriculum in her program for three- to five-year-old children, which includes children with disabilities. She has also worked with the Hope School Summer Camp Program for several years.

Emily Sedgwick Galvin taught preschool for 10 years and earned her master's degree in Child Development at Northern Illinois University. She is a part-time instructor at the College of DuPage (Glen Ellyn, Illinois) and a naturalist guide and instructor at the Morton Arboretum (Lisle, Illinois). Ms.Galvin developed and coor dinates the Arboretum's preschool outreach program. She conducts in-service teacher nature workshops and recently published an article, "The Joy of Seasons," in the May/June 1994 issue of Young Children.

Marti Harmon is the founder and director of the Young Naturalist Center in Los Angeles, California, which offers an early childhood multicultural environmental education program. Dr. Harmon assisted in the development of a curriculum guide with the Rosebud Sioux Tribe Head Start program and a multicultural environmental education program for the Latin American Civic Association Head Start program. Dr. Harmon is currently interested in working collaboratively on teacher training and program development projects, especially as these relate to multicultural perspectives in early childhood environmental education. Dr. Harmon can be contacted at the Young Naturalist Center, 12725 Landale Street, Studio City, CA 91604. Phone 818/761-3008.

Robert E. Holtz is a professor of Biology and Science Education at Concordia College in St.Paul, Minnesota. He holds a master 's degree in Zoology and a doctorate in Environmental Education. His publications include numerous articles relating to science education, teacher training, attitudes in environmental education, and stewardship. Dr. Holtz also developed an Environmental Education Program Planning Guide for the Minnesota Department of Education.

Susan Hopkins is the assistant director of the Cal State University Children's Center. She is also the coeditor of Discover the World: Empowering Children to Value Themselves, Others and the Earth, a peace education curriculum manual published by New Society Publishers (1990). She was awarded the 1990 Peace Award by Concerned Educators Allied for a Safe Environment (CEASE) and is a frequent presenter and workshop leader for professional conferences and university classes.

Mavis Lewis-Webber is an early childhood environmental education consultant in Canada. She received funding from Health & Welfare Canada to develop Earthcycles: Environmental Education with Preschool Children. This publication has been distributed to preschool facilities across Canada. Ms. Lewis-Webber has presented Earthcycles at provincial and national early childhood conferences. She also sits on the Province of Manitoba Steering Committee on Early Years Environmental Education.

Pamela A. Mowbray received a bachelor of science in Recreation Studies with a major in Outdoor Education from Ohio University in Athens, Ohio. She currently works as a naturalist for the Johnny Appleseed Metropolitan Park District in Lima, Ohio, and has worked as a preschool teacher for several years while pursuing her career as a naturalist. She enjoys planning and presenting a wide variety of environmental and nature interpretation programs for the general public.

Marcie Oltman has a master's degree in Environmental Education and Interpretation and is currently working on a second master's in Early Childhood Education. For three years she served as director of Children's Programs at the New Canaan Nature Center in New Canaan, Connecticut, and directed the Beginner's Nature Program, an early childhood environmental education program at this center. Ms. Oltman has planned and conducted numerous workshops for parents, teachers, and other professionals.

Linda Penn, sometimes referred to as "The Butterfly Lady," is creator and coordinator of the Natural and Environmental Science Program for Lourdes College in Sylvania, Ohio. She also coordinates educational programs at the Toledo Botanical Gardens, including a summer science camp. Ms. Penn is the author of 12 books for young children in the "Young Scientists' Explore" series, the coauthor of a kindergarten science curriculum, and coproducer of "Sing-A-Long Science" tapes featuring seasonal themes. Butterflies and moths are at the heart of Ms. Penn's teaching. She uses these wonders of nature to foster a sense of wonder, love, and respect for the world of nature.

Adelia Peters is a professor in the College of Education at Bowling Green State University (BGSU) in Bowling Green, Ohio. For several years, she was director of the Center for Environmental Programs at BGSU and currently serves as the advisor for students in the College of Education majoring in Environmental Science. Dr. Peters has worked closely with Dr. Wilson in the "Environmental Education for Preschoolers" project at BGSU.

Janice Sheffield is head teacher at the Cal State Fullerton Children's Center and a contributor to the book <u>Discover the World: Empowering Children to Value Themselves, Others, and the Earth</u>, a peace education curriculum manual published by New Society Publishers (1990).

Daniella Tilbury is a professor in the Department of Education at the University of Cambridge in the United Kingdom. Her doctoral dissertation focused on developing a model for initial teacher training in environmental education, and her current publications address a variety of environmental education issues. Dr. Tilbury is currently involved with researching environmental education in the later primary years and developing in-service courses for teachers at this level. She is also working on developing the "grounded theory" research methodology in ways that will enhance educational research. Dr. Tilbury serves as a consultant to the Gibraltar government, where she is developing a national policy and teacher support networks for Gibraltarian teachers.

Eleanor W. Tinto is a retired teacher, a former teacher and principal in religious education, a volunteer at the Louisiana Nature and Science Center, an ombudsman program visitor in nursing homes, a member of Church Women United, president of a senior citizen group, and member of an interfaith group in New Orleans working to better the city and the environment. Mrs. Tinto is married (42 years) and has 9 children and 11 grandchildren.

Kelly J. Warren has a master's degree in Environmental Science with emphasis in freshwater resources. She is also a registered nurse. Ms.W arren currently works as an environmental education research specialist at the University of Wisconsin-Extension, Madison, Wisconsin, and as a naturalist at the University of Wisconsin-Arboretum. She writes for Madison's community radio station, WORT, on various local topics including education, health, and environmental issues. Past environmental education experience includes working as the Nature Program director at Bradford Woods Outdoor Recreation Center in Martinsville, Indiana.

Marina Williford is an early childhood special education teacher for the Wood County Schools in Ohio. She has recently completed a master's degree in Early Childhood Special Education at Bowling Green State University in Bowling Green, Ohio.

Ruth Wilson is a professor at Bowling Green State University in Bowling Green, Ohio. She teaches graduate courses in the area of early childhood special education and has been coordinating a number of different projects in early childhood environmental education. Dr. Wilson is the author of <u>Fostering a Sense of Wonder during the Early Childhood Years</u>, a curriculum guide designed to infuse environmental education into all aspects of a preschool program. Dr. Wilson has also published numerous articles on early childhood environmental education and conducts workshops and seminars on the topic.